First and Second Thessalonians

INTERPRETATION
A Bible Commentary for Teaching and Preaching

INTERPRETATION
A BIBLE COMMENTARY FOR TEACHING AND PREACHING

James Luther Mays, *Editor*
Patrick D. Miller, *Old Testament Editor*
Paul J. Achtemeier, *New Testament Editor*

BEVERLY ROBERTS GAVENTA

First and Second Thessalonians

INTERPRETATION

A Bible Commentary
for Teaching and Preaching

John Knox Press
LOUISVILLE

Library of Congress Cataloging-in-Publication Data

Gaventa, Beverly Roberts.
  First and Second Thessalonians / Beverly Roberts Gaventa.
      p.   cm. — (Interpretation, a Bible commentary for teaching and preaching)
    Includes bibliographical references.
    ISBN 0-8042-3142-7 (alk. paper)
    1. Bible. N.T. Thessalonians—Commentaries. I. Title. II. Series.
    BS2725.3.G38   1998
    227'.81077—dc21   97-30706

© copyright John Knox Press 1998
This book is printed on acid-free paper that meets the American National Standards Institute Z39.48 standard. ♾
98 99 00 01 02 03 04 05 06 07—10 9 8 7 6 5 4 3 2 1
Printed in the United States of America
John Knox Press
Louisville, Kentucky

For Bill

SERIES PREFACE

This series of commentaries offers an interpretation of the books of the Bible. It is designed to meet the needs of students, teachers, ministers, and priests for a contemporary expository commentary. These volumes will not replace the historical critical commentary or homiletical aids to preaching. The purpose of this series is rather to provide a third kind of resource, a commentary which presents the integrated result of historical and theological work with the biblical text.

An interpretation in the full sense of the term involves a text, an interpreter, and someone for whom the interpretation is made. Here, the text is what stands written in the Bible in its full identity as literature from the time of "the prophets and apostles," the literature which is read to inform, inspire, and guide the life of faith. The interpreters are scholars who seek to create an interpretation which is both faithful to the text and useful to the church. The series is written for those who teach, preach, and study the Bible in the community of faith.

The comment generally takes the form of expository essays. It is planned and written in the light of the needs and questions which arise in the use of the Bible as Holy Scripture. The insights and results of contemporary scholarly research are used for the sake of the exposition. The commentators write as exegetes and theologians. The task which they undertake is both to deal with what the texts say and to discern their meaning for faith and life. The exposition is the unified work of one interpreter.

The text on which the comment is based is the Revised Standard Version of the Bible and, since its appearance, the New Revised Standard Version. The general availability of these translations makes the printing of a text in the commentary unnecessary. The commentators have also had other current versions in view as they worked and refer to their readings where it is helpful. The text is divided into sections appropriate to the particular book; comment deals with passages as a whole, rather than proceeding word by word, or verse by verse.

Writers have planned their volumes in light of the requirements set by the exposition of the book assigned to them. Biblical books differ in character, content, and arrangement. They also differ in the way they have been and are used in the liturgy, thought, and devotion of the church. The distinctiveness and use of particular books have been taken into account in decisions about the approach, emphasis, and use of space in the commentaries. The goal has been to allow writers to develop the format which provides for the best presentation of their interpretation.

The result, writers and editors hope, is a commentary which both explains and applies, an interpretation which deals with both the meaning and the significance of biblical texts. Each commentary reflects, of course, the writer's own approach and perception of the church and world. It could and should not be otherwise. Every interpretation of any kind is individual in that sense; it is one reading of the text. But all who work at the interpretation of Scripture in the church need the help and stimulation of a colleague's reading and understanding of the text. If these volumes serve and encourage interpretation in that way, their preparation and publication will realize their purpose.

The Editors

PREFACE

Pastors often tell me that they find preaching from the letters of Paul particularly difficult. This commentary on the Thessalonian correspondence reflects not only my own persistent preoccupation with Pauline texts but my conviction that, however challenging they are to interpreters, these letters offer each generation crucial reminders about the radically offensive nature of God's grace, as well as direction for the care and feeding of pastors and Christian churches. My hope is that pastors and teachers will find in this volume encouragement for their ministries as well as guidance in the reading of these letters.

My students have played a large role in the shaping of this commentary. I especially wish to thank those who participated in my 1996 course on the Thessalonian correspondence, whose diverse interests included text criticism, the insights of Chrysostom, the quest for the "most important" passage, and the terrors of preaching. They will not find all their questions answered here, and certainly not answered to their liking, but I hope they will recognize that their ideas and concerns have enlivened this volume.

I am grateful to James L. Mays and Paul J. Achtemeier, both for the initial invitation to write this commentary and for their encouragement throughout the process. It is a pleasure to work with such experienced scholars and editors. C. Clifton Black, Charles B. Cousar, Victor Paul Furnish, E. Elizabeth Johnson, and J. Louis Martyn all assisted with conversation, bibliography, and the thoughtful question posed at the right time. Patrick J. Willson read and commented on the manuscript, but he also complicated my task with frequent, pointed reminders that I was writing for pastors first and foremost. I appreciate the assistance of David Freedholm, who made available to me his extensive bibliography on 1 Thessalonians, as well as Michael Daise and William S. Campbell for help with bibliographical details. In addition, William S. Campbell read a complete draft of the manuscript and thereby saved me numerous errors. As much as I might wish it otherwise, it is clear that the flaws remaining in this book are my own.

This volume is dedicated to my husband, William C. Gaventa, who did not convert an illegible draft into typescript, correct my grammar and spelling, or transform our home into a haven from the outside world. What he did do, as he has done now for half his life, is tend to his labors and respect the need I have for my own. That is a rare gift, and one for which I am ever grateful.

CONTENTS

THE BOOK OF

First Thessalonians

Introduction

If our ancient predecessors in the Christian faith had arranged the New Testament writings according to their dates of composition, 1 Thessalonians would stand at the beginning in place of the Gospel of Matthew. At least by the reckoning of most New Testament scholars, Paul wrote the letter we know as 1 Thessalonians around 51 C.E., which makes it the earliest Christian writing and, indeed, the earliest evidence we possess for the existence of Christianity.

Despite the historic significance of 1 Thessalonians, however, it has been a neglected gem among the letters of Paul. It was not because of their reading of 1 Thessalonians that Augustine and Luther broke with their theological predecessors. Nor has this letter served as the battleground for decisions about the ordination of women or the nature of the Eucharist. Even its words of assurance for the grieving find themselves upstaged in most funeral litanies by the better-known lines of Romans 8 or 1 Corinthians 15.

This very lack of familiarity makes 1 Thessalonians an ideal place to begin discovering, or perhaps rediscovering, the letters of Paul. The letter does not bear so many doctrinal issues in its wake that we can scarcely hear the text for hearing those other debates. This letter also has about it the virtue of brevity. It can be consumed in a single sitting—and a short one at that—making it the perfect text for the sound bite age.

1 Thessalonians is not only accessible, however; it is profoundly pastoral. In the opening lines of the letter, Paul uses the familiar

1

language of faith, hope, and love, although he does so in an unfamiliar way: "your work of faith and labor of love and steadfastness of hope in our Lord Jesus Christ" (1:3). Those three phrases nicely anticipate the letter's content. Here Paul recalls the way in which faith in the gospel of Jesus Christ came alive in one city (1:2–10). He pours out the apostles' love for this group of believers and urges that same love as a prime feature of this new community of believers (2:17—3:10). And he identifies the community by its confident hope in the triumphant return of Jesus Christ (1:9–12; 3:13; 4:13—5:11; 5:23).

These three themes form a prism through which Paul examines and then addresses a variety of concerns. Paul views the suffering of the Thessalonians and their separation from the apostles in the larger context of conflict between the God who calls and sustains and Satan who endeavors to destroy. He comforts the grieving with the promise that all believers will again be together when they are gathered to the returning and triumphant Jesus Christ. He offers ethical admonitions that build up the boundaries around this fledgling community, boundaries of love and respect that protect the community but also maintain its attractiveness to others.

The Author and Audience

My family and I live at 175 Alexander Street. Occasionally, however, we receive mail intended for someone at 175 Andrews Street. We have never met the resident at 175 Andrews, but we know a number of things about her. We know her name, the college she attended (from alumni magazines), the general area of her work (from professional journals), and perhaps even her political leanings (from the solicitations of various organizations). We also suspect her of being thoughtful, since she once left a stack of *our* misdirected mail at the back door. All of this we surmise from evidence bestowed in our mailbox, without attempting to contact her or employing circuitous and unscrupulous methods (such as sorting through her garbage or interrogating her neighbors).

This innocuous reconstruction has a counterpart in our reading of early Christian letters. As we begin reading Paul's letter to believers in Thessalonica, clues in the letter help us identify the author of the letter, its intended audience, and something of the relationship between them. The letter opens by identifying the writers as Paul, Silvanus, and Timothy, although later in the letter Paul speaks alone (2:18; 3:5), suggesting that his voice dominates. Unlike the questions that plague the interpretation of 2 Thessalonians (see Introduction to Second Thessalonians), the authorship of 1 Thessalonians remains uncontested.

The letter allows us to deduce certain things about the audience.

2

It consists primarily, if not entirely, of Gentiles who have become believers in Israel's God and in Jesus as God's son. The early lines of the letter make this clear, as Paul recalls how the Thessalonians "turned to God from idols" (1:9), a description of conversion that would be inappropriate for Jews. Later, in the ethical admonitions, Paul warns the audience against the "lustful passion" of those "Gentiles who do not know God" (4:5); by contrast, the Thessalonians to whom he writes are Gentiles who *do* know God. In addition, the harsh polemic of 2:14–16 against the Jews (or Judeans) is difficult to imagine if Paul is addressing a group of Jewish Christians or even a group consisting of both Gentile and Jewish Christians.

Whatever we can learn about Thessalonica itself may add texture and shading to our general portrait of the audience of this first Christian letter. A contemporary sermon for a Christian congregation in Washington would differ from one for Detroit or Cape Town. In the same way, Paul's letter surely reflects the social, political, and religious situation of Thessalonica. Discerning the details of that situation and the lines it etches in the portrait, however, is a delicate undertaking because of the paucity of our sources and their chronological distance from us.

By the time Paul wrote, Thessalonica had been under Roman rule for over two centuries, although culturally it remained a Greek city. As the capital of the province of Macedonia and thus the seat of Roman administration, Thessalonica had a certain political significance. Because it was a port city and was located on a major Roman highway, the Via Egnetia, its residents would have been exposed to a wide variety of social and cultural influences.

Typical of the religious life of the period throughout most of the Roman Empire, the Thessalonians honored many deities. Among those most prominent were the Greek god Dionysus; the Egyptian deities Isis, Osiris, and Serapis; and the Phrygian god Cabirus. Thessalonica also participated in the imperial cult, probably as early as the end of the first century B.C.E. Scholars debate the relative importance of these religious practices and especially the ways in which Paul may be responding to them in his letter (e.g., does the sexual imagery associated with some of these practices have anything to do with Paul's warning about sexual misconduct in 4:3–8?). At the very least, such lively and varied religious practices make it clear that the Thessalonians were hardly impoverished when it came to religious options, as Christians sometimes depict the world prior to the advent of Christianity.

Paul, Silvanus, and Timothy brought what many would have viewed as merely one more religious option into this bustling, cosmopolitan

3

city. They worked for their own sustenance (1 Thess. 2:9), but on more than one occasion they received assistance from believers in Philippi (Phil. 4:15–16), which suggests that their stay in Thessalonica was an extended one.

Some among the Thessalonians responded to their instruction. Nothing in the letter permits us to estimate how many "turned to God" or under what circumstances. Later, something forced the apostles to leave the city. Despite their efforts to return, by the time he writes this letter Paul has not been able to do so. While he waits in Athens, he sends Timothy back to Thessalonica. Timothy returns with an encouraging report, and the report in turn gives rise to the letter.

Many will wish to supplement this slender sketch by immediately opening the pages of the Acts of the Apostles, where Luke presents a strikingly different picture of Paul's mission to Thessalonica. According to Acts 17, Paul and Silas begin their stay in Thessalonica by going to the synagogue. They preach in the synagogue over the course of three Sabbaths, and in response both Jews and Gentiles become believers. However, certain Jews become jealous of this success and "set the city in an uproar" (17:5), as a result of which a believer named Jason is attacked and led before the civil authorities, where he and the others are charged with "turning the world upside down" (17:6).

Fearful for the safety of Paul and Silas, the Thessalonian believers send them off to Beroea that same night. There they continue their mission until Thessalonian Jews arrive to make trouble in Beroea as well. Paul is dispatched to Athens, but Silas and Timothy remain behind in Beroea.

Already we see difficulties in reconciling these two accounts. Luke says nothing of Timothy's presence in Thessalonica nor of a return visit there by Timothy, and Silas/Silvanus remains with Timothy rather than with Paul (as in 1 Thess. 3:1–2, 6). Luke's story about Jason has no counterpart in the letter. The most important difference between the two, however, is that Luke places both the work of the apostles and the resulting disturbance in the context of a synagogue, while the letter itself gives no indication of a synagogue setting, Jewish converts in this city, or Jewish resistance to Christian preaching.

Luke's narrative is attractive and familiar, but he writes several decades after Paul's sojourn in Thessalonica. Here, as often in Acts, Luke's treatment of Paul differs sharply from the glimpses of Paul that emerge from his own letters, and it is by no means clear that Luke knew Paul or had access to eyewitness information about him. For those reasons, it is best to privilege the bits and pieces of information we can tease out of the letters and to introduce Luke's narrative only with great

4

caution. The practice in this commentary will be to draw on Acts only to supplement the letter and only when Luke's account does not conflict with Paul's.

The Form and Purpose of 1 Thessalonians

Despite the relative neglect of 1 Thessalonians, scholars have recently engaged in heated debate that bears significantly on the purpose of the letter. A debate about the purpose of this letter may seem strange. On first reading, many assume that Paul is engaged in sheer self-defense. Once we move beyond the opening lines of the letter, Paul moves immediately to language that sounds highly apologetic:

> For our appeal does not spring from deceit or impure motives or trickery. . . . [W]e never came with words of flattery or with a pretext for greed; nor did we seek praise from mortals, whether from you or from others.
>
> (1 Thess. 2:3, 5–6)

Perhaps the most natural conclusion to draw from these remarks, at least for readers in the late twentieth century, is that Paul writes in order to defend himself. To ears attuned to the incessant public discourse of accusation and denial, Paul sounds very much like someone charged with profiteering from his preaching and perhaps with abandoning the Thessalonians (see, for example, 2:17—3:5). We quickly conclude that he writes to clear his own name and reestablish the relationship with the Thessalonians.

As the commentary that follows will suggest, there are difficulties with this explanation, however attractive it may be at first glance (see below on 1 Thess. 2:1–12). Scholars who have explored the conventions of letter writing and persuasive public discourse (or rhetoric) in the ancient world agree that 1 Thessalonians is not a letter of self-defense.

Beyond that single point of convergence, however, there is little agreement on the precise form, and therefore the purpose, of 1 Thessalonians. Drawing on ancient letter-writing theory and practice, some scholars argue that the letter has the form and purpose of a "paraenetic letter" or letter of exhortation. Based on the close friendship between himself and the Thessalonians, Paul writes to offer his own conduct as an example to be imitated (chapters 1—3) and to give advice on a variety of topics (chapters 4—5).

Rhetorical analysis, the study of strategies of persuasion in discourse, prompts other scholars to argue that 1 Thessalonians is an epideictic letter, that is, a letter that praises or blames someone for

5

convictions or behavior. These scholars point to such epideictic features as Paul's praise of God for all that God has done among the Thessalonians (1:2–15), his praise of himself for his exemplary conduct (2:2b–8), and his praise of the Thessalonians and their behavior (1:6–10; 2:14; 4:9; 5:1–2).

Still other scholars, again employing the tools of classical rhetorical analysis, view the rhetoric of 1 Thessalonians as deliberative. Deliberative rhetoric involves persuading an audience to take a particular action in the future. Paul seeks to persuade the Thessalonians to persist in their chosen course of faithfulness (3:6–13), to choose a particular set of behaviors (4:2–12), and to avoid others (5:15).

The questions raised by this debate bear significantly on the reading and therefore on the preaching and teaching of this letter, although it may seem otherwise at first glance. That becomes apparent if we think in terms of contemporary letter-writing practices. "I write to thank you for your generous support" may introduce a letter thanking a dear friend who has offered comfort in a difficult time. On the other hand, those very same words could also introduce a letter from a college or university development officer, someone who knows only that the computer indicates the addressee contributed to the Annual Fund last year and might do so again this year. Other than a few words or phrases, the two letters will have almost nothing in common; confusing the two would require willful misreading.

Unfortunately, discerning whether 1 Thessalonians is a paraenetic letter, an example of deliberative or epideictic rhetoric, or something else entirely is far more difficult than distinguishing between letters of thanks and solicitations. The debate about the purpose of 1 Thessalonians involves several highly technical and complex questions, such as the nature of ancient epistolary theory, the extent to which rhetorical practice obtained in letter writing, the extent to which any rhetorical artifact ever offered a "pure" example of a rhetorical genre, and the sorts of evidence that should be regarded as relevant for understanding rhetorical practice. Beyond these technical matters, judgments about the particular form and purpose of the letter also involve a reader's grasp of the letter as a whole; that is, readers come to a conclusion about this matter as they read and reread the letter.

My own assessment, which admittedly runs the risk of oversimplifying these technical questions, is that the primary purpose of 1 Thessalonians is consolidation or, to use Paul's own language, "upbuilding" (see, for example, 1 Thess. 5:11; 1 Cor. 10:23; 14:12; 14:26; 2 Cor. 2:19; Rom. 14:19; 15:2). This suggestion borrows elements from several of

6

the positions sketched above, and especially from Thomas Olbricht's suggestion that 1 Thessalonians reflects the rhetoric of "reconfirmation" ("An Aristotelian Rhetorical Analysis of 1 Thessalonians"). Having received the report of Timothy about the continuing faithfulness of the Thessalonians, Paul writes to consolidate or confirm that faithfulness. He does so by recalling the initial visit he and his coworkers made to Thessalonica and the close personal relationships they established, by celebrating the response of the Thessalonians to the gospel of Jesus Christ, and by urging behavior that marks the Christian community as distinctive but not closed. All of these concerns he locates firmly in the realm of God's power, a power that brings faith into existence and will sustain believers until and beyond the return of Jesus Christ.

**The Structure
of the Letter**

Exactly how does the letter accomplish this task of consolidation? How does Paul structure his argument? Once again, a question that seems straightforward becomes complicated. Like his contemporaries, Paul generally included a thanksgiving in his letters, immediately following the opening salutation. With 1 Thessalonians, however, the first half of the letter is so steeped in the language of thanksgiving and praise that it is difficult to decide where the thanksgiving proper ends and the body of the letter begins.

The following analysis of the structure of 1 Thessalonians should assist readers in seeing roughly the movement of the letter:

Salutation	1:1
Thanksgiving	1:2–10
Body	2:1—3:13
Conduct of the Apostles	2:1–16
Separation and Reassurance	2:17—3:10
Concluding Prayer	3:11–13
Ethical Instruction	4:1—5:24
Concerning Community Boundaries	4:1–12
Concerning the Return of the Lord	4:13—5:11
Concerning Conduct within the Community	5:12–22
Concluding Prayer	5:23–24
Closing	5:25–28

Although this analysis may facilitate reading the letter, Paul's exuberance overflows the structure. The break between 1:10 and 2:1 is far

7

less significant than this structure suggests, since Paul moves gracefully between the Thessalonians' response to the gospel (1:6–10) and the apostles' behavior during their initial encounter (2:1–16). In addition, a strict analysis of letter form might identify the prayer of 5:23–24 as part of the letter closing rather than as part of the ethical instruction.

On the other hand, this analysis of the letter's structure underscores the way in which prayerful thanksgiving dominates 1 Thessalonians. All three major sections of the letter conclude with prayer. The thanksgiving itself (1:2–10) *is* a prayer. The body of the letter culminates with the prayer of 3:11–13. And the ethical instruction ends with prayer (5:23–24). In addition, each of those prayers shares a preoccupation with the return of Jesus (1:10; 3:13; 4:23). By drawing attention to the thanksgiving and the prayers, this reading of the structure of 1 Thessalonians highlights something important about the letter: here Paul consolidates believers in Thessalonica in their faith as they stand before the God who has called them into faith and who can be trusted to preserve them at the triumphant return of Jesus Christ.

[*Note:* The divisions in the commentary diverge slightly from this analysis by connecting the prayers (at 3:11–13 and 5:23–24) with the sections preceding them. That divergence reflects the desire to comment on the prayers as they interpret what precedes, rather than rigidly follow letter structure.]

The Reading of a Letter

Paul concludes this first Christian writing with the solemn commandment that the letter must be read to all believers in Thessalonica. As Raymond Collins has observed, these instructions changed the church's existence (*Birth of the New Testament*, 210). However unintentionally, by adopting the practice of reading this letter in the context of the gathered community—and the letters and Gospels that followed it—the church entered into a permanent relationship with this text. Eventually, the writing of a single letter to a small and specific group of Christians gave birth to the canonization of the whole New Testament for the whole church.

Presumably the Thessalonians read Paul's letters because they remembered him and his coworkers with gratitude and because they anticipated that his letter would assist them in their faith. But contemporary Christians, lacking the firsthand experience of the Thessalonians, may well wonder why we should continue to read this letter. What profit may be derived from it for the present? The commentary that follows will identify the issues Paul addresses in this letter as issues that are very much alive and well two millennia after its composition.

8

For example, one difficulty that pervades the church concerns the nature of its ministry and the relationship between the church and its ministers. Paul's recollections about the time he and Silvanus and Timothy spent in Thessalonica and the depth of emotion in those recollections might be instructive for a church that seems in danger of treating its ministers like disposable commodities. Extended reflection on the emotional toil involved in pastoral ministry might challenge congregations to be more supportive of their pastors.

Another way in which 1 Thessalonians proves challenging is through Paul's forthright insistence that human conduct is answerable to God. Paul shares with other biblical witnesses a conviction that humanity exists to please God. That conviction will make many uncomfortable, accustomed as we are to trimming our ethical sails to meet our own desires and each day's winds. But it could scarcely be more timely.

Perhaps the most important issue that makes this letter timely is its disarming awareness of God. First Thessalonians is about faith, love, and hope, not as human attributes but as gifts that spring from God alone. It is God who calls into faith, God who enables human love, and God toward whom hope is directed. Reading the letter, then, may serve to enable Christians today to use the word "God" without blushing, to think theologically about our lives and our endeavors.

As we turn from these questions of introduction to our engagement with the letter itself, the question of *how* we read becomes urgent. Many people bring to Scripture an exalted view of it that, ironically, defeats their genuine engagement with the text even before they begin. In his classic guide, *How to Read a Book,* Mortimer Adler conceded that there is one occasion when people do know how to read:

> When they are in love and are reading a love letter, they read for all they are worth. They read every word three ways; they read between the lines and in the margins; they read the whole in terms of the parts, and each part in terms of the whole; they grow sensitive to context and ambiguity, to insinuation and implication; they perceive the color of words, the odor of phrases, and the weight of sentences. They may even take the punctuation into account. Then, if never before or after, they read. (14)

Adler's words point us to an appropriate reading of this letter. Paul writes a kind of love letter, one in which he pours out his own love for the Thessalonians, while sustaining himself with the knowledge that they love him as well. Most important, he acknowledges that their mutual love derives from God's own love for all.

9

Commentary on
First Thessalonians

Consider the images invoked by mentioning the apostle Paul. Perhaps it is a street-corner evangelist, tugging at sleeves and shouting after passersby in Corinth. Or is Paul pacing the floor, struggling to find the right words for a letter to Christians at Philippi? Perhaps the Paul who comes to mind has taken up residence in a prison cell in Ephesus or Jerusalem or Rome. Whatever his activity and location in our imagination, one dominant image of Paul is that of an early Christian soloist, a virtuoso apostle roaming the ancient Mediterranean world in search of potential converts. On this scenario, his companions, if there are such, slip far into the background, and the Christian communities Paul initiates are little more than passive receptacles for his preaching.

This image owes much to the high regard Christians have had for Paul's letters and to Luke's stories in the Acts of the Apostles, but it also overlooks important elements in Paul's letters. Even in the first verses of 1 Thessalonians, a different picture of Paul emerges. Here Paul is by no means a solo performer. He is part of a team, as is clear from the initial verse of the letter. More important, here Paul speaks of evangelism as something that transforms both evangelist and evangelized (vv. 2–10; see also 2:1–12).

"Grace to You and Peace"

1 THESSALONIANS 1:1

Little in the opening of a letter catches our attention. At most, we may quickly check to see that it bears our name instead of that of another family member or a neighbor. We rush past the greeting and opening lines to discover what is actually at stake. Does this letter concern a family in turmoil, a bill unpaid, an illness diagnosed? Given modern epistolary conventions, such haste may be understandable, but reading the opening of biblical letters with the same dispatch creates serious problems. The salutation (1:1) provides important clues about

10

the persons involved in the letter, their relationships, and their locations. It invites us to read the letter through the eyes of those persons and their ongoing conversation with one another.

Even from the meager wording of this initial greeting, we can detect evidence of a good deal of unfinished business between the senders of this letter and the "church of the Thessalonians." As the letter unfolds, we learn that Paul, Silvanus, and Timothy together made an initial visit to Thessalonica, where they preached and taught the gospel of Jesus Christ. Some Thessalonians (we have no way of ascertaining how many) "turned to God from idols" (1:9) and joined these apostles in their expectation of the return of God's son, Jesus Christ. Following the apostles' departure, Paul found himself unable to go back to Thessalonica (2:17–20) and sent Timothy to learn how the Thessalonian believers were faring. He has now returned to Paul and Silvanus, and it is Timothy's news that appears to prompt the writing of the letter. (This sketch of the letter's comments stands in tension with the story in Acts 17, but priority will be given to Paul's letters in adjudicating these details; see Introduction, and see commentary on 2:17—3:10.)

Whatever the historical events surrounding the writing of this letter, it is important to notice the presence of all three names in the salutation. The naming of these three persons might mean that all three took part in the composition of the letter (that 1 Thessalonians was written by committee?), but later it seems evident that the strongest voice is that of Paul (see 2:18; 3:5; 5:27). Whatever the facts of composition, the introduction of the gospel in Thessalonica was not the work of a single individual but of a team. Not only do Silvanus and Timothy join Paul in sending the letter, but they joined Paul in the initial work in Thessalonica (1:2—2:12) and continue in profound concern for the ongoing life of the Christian community in that place (2:17—3:10). As surprising as it will be to those accustomed to the specialized meaning of the term "apostle" elsewhere in the New Testament, all three are referred to in 2:7 as "apostles of Christ" (see on 2:1–12).

The recipients of the letter are identified simply as "the church of the Thessalonians." Since we associate the word "church" with structured organizations that go well beyond the local community, it might be better to think of the Greek word *ekklēsia* as a "gathering" or an "association." The phrase "of the Thessalonians" is distinctive, since the later Pauline letters address the church "*in* Corinth" or "the churches *of* Galatia." This phrase also reinforces the translation "association"; the

11

letter addresses the group of Thessalonians who have come to share the senders' convictions about Jesus Christ.

The next phrase raises a number of questions. Does "in God the Father and the Lord Jesus Christ" describe the church itself (that is, the church has its location in God and Jesus), or does it describe Paul, Silvanus, and Timothy, who write by means of God and Jesus Christ? The Greek can be translated either way. And what are we to make of the relationship between "God the Father" and "the Lord Jesus Christ"? Are the titles "Father" and "Lord" synonymous? Does "Father" here refer to God as the father of Jesus Christ or as the father of all creatures? Such subtle distinctions quickly grow dizzying for many readers. Far more important than resolving them is lingering over the too obvious but often neglected point: God and Jesus Christ are the primary agents in the Thessalonian church. Whatever Paul, Silvanus, and Timothy began, whatever the Thessalonians themselves have accomplished, it is God who is to be thanked (1:2), God who directs and strengthens the church (3:11–13), God who is and will remain faithful (5:24). The letter reveals much about the relationship between the apostles and the Thessalonians, and it has much to suggest about relationships among Christians in the present, but none of that can be understood apart from "God the Father and the Lord Jesus Christ."

Even in this, the earliest of his letters, Paul departs somewhat from the letter style conventional in his time. Instead of completing the salutation with "Greetings," Paul writes "Grace to you and peace" (see also Rom. 1:7; 1 Cor. 1:3; 2 Cor. 1:3; Gal. 1:3; Phil. 1:2; Philemon 3). Whether intentional or not, the alteration is significant. Although there are many elements of friendship in this letter, it is not merely a letter from friends to friends, as the word "greeting" might imply. This particular friendship comes into being by virtue of the action of God in Jesus Christ, the same God whose promises include grace and peace.

Verse 1 deserves our sustained attention, then, not simply because it provides us with historical lenses through which to read what follows. Without going even a single line further, we know already that this association, however much it may gather like-minded people, is not in the first instance a social event, a civic club, or a philanthropic organization. It exists only in relationship to "God the Father and the Lord Jesus Christ." Few sermons would confine themselves to a single verse in a letter salutation, yet this one offers an important reminder about who the church is.

12

A Profusion of Thanksgiving

1 THESSALONIANS 1:2–10

Conforming to the letter-writing conventions of his day, Paul's letters routinely include a thanksgiving. Only when he writes to the Galatians does Paul omit any word of thanks, presumably because events in the Galatian churches have so distressed him that he cannot recall any grounds for thanksgiving. In a sense, this letter to the Thessalonians presents the opposite problem; there is more thanksgiving here than interpreters know how to handle. It is a simple matter to identify the beginning of the thanksgiving in 1:2, but the end of the thanksgiving proves elusive. In Greek, 1:2–5 constitutes one long sentence in which the main verb is "we give thanks," so that the most narrow definition of the thanksgiving would identify verse 5 as the conclusion. Yet verses 6–10 follow so naturally from and are so directly connected with verses 1–5 that the thanksgiving surely runs through at least 1:10. Another section of thanksgiving appears in 2:13–16, and a brief word of thanks appears also in 3:9; in fact, some analyses of the letter identify the thanksgiving as 1:2—2:16 or even 1:2—3:9.

Reading and interpreting the text does not depend on answering this technical question about letter structure, of course, but the profusion of thanksgiving in this letter reveals something essential. The arrival of the gospel among the Thessalonians is an event for which thanksgiving is a primary response.

Even at the outset of the thanksgiving, we notice its effusiveness. When Paul contends that he and Silvanus and Timothy "always" give thanks for and "constantly" remember the Thessalonians, we are inclined to be skeptical (see the similar expressions in 1 Cor. 1:4; Phil. 1:4; Philemon 1:4). How is it possible to pray always and constantly? There may be more than a little hyperbole at work here, but these assertions take on a different tone if we listen to them in the context of the familial imagery that characterizes the letter. Although we will see that those images are varied, prominent among them is the assumption that Paul and his coworkers became parents to the Thessalonians. Paul affirms that he and his coworkers behaved toward the Thessalonians "like a nurse tenderly caring for her own children" (2:7) and "like a father with his children" (2:11). These claims make Paul's assertions about constant

13

prayer more credible. One of the fearsome realities of many parents' experience is that children are never removed from their parents' thoughts, certainly never from their hearts. If prayer involves those "sighs too deep for words" (Rom. 8:26), as Paul will later write, then there is a sense in which parents always are in prayer. If Paul finds himself regarding the Thessalonians as his children, something more than rhetorical flourish is at work when he claims to remember the Thessalonians "constantly."

The Table of Contents (v. 3)

Thanksgivings in the Pauline letters also provide an implicit table of contents for the letter that follows. For example, in 1 Corinthians Paul mentions the fact that the Corinthians have been enriched "in speech and knowledge of every kind" and in spiritual gifts (1 Cor. 1:4–7). In the body of the letter, he returns to these topics that have become problematic among believers in Corinth.

In this particular thanksgiving, Paul celebrates the Thessalonians' "work of faith and labor of love and steadfastness of hope in our Lord Jesus Christ." Given the utter familiarity of the triad "faith, hope, and love" from 1 Corinthians 13, those words seem to leap off the page. Yet here they do not appear in conventional order, or what seems *to us* conventional order (see also Rom. 5:1–5). Instead of "faith, hope, and love" we find "faith, love, and hope." More important, each of these attributes is introduced and governed by another term: "work of faith," "labor of love," and "steadfastness of hope in our Lord Jesus Christ." It is tempting to skip over the introductory terms as so much embroidery, familiar religious rhetoric, but they are essential hints to the content of the letter to come.

The expression "work of faith" is awkward in English, and the Greek might be better captured with a phrase such as "work that stems from faith" or "work that belongs to faith." Although it cannot be restricted to one section of the letter, this phrase nicely anticipates 1:6—2:16, where Paul recalls his initial visit to Thessalonica and the way in which the Thessalonians received the gospel.

"Labor of love" is an evocative expression, one that has come to be applied to an endless number of endeavors undertaken for the sheer pleasure of labor or out of affection for another. Gardening in this sense can be a "labor of love," but so can the family laundry (at least in theory). The Thessalonians are engaged in a labor of love in the sense that their life in the present embodies Christian love. They are to love one another (3:11–13; 4:9–12) and conduct themselves in a manner consistent with that love (4:1–8; 5:12–22).

"Steadfastness of hope" is perhaps the phrase easiest to underinterpret, especially if we hear it as part of the familiar triad of "faith, hope, and love." The problem arises when hope becomes a Christian virtue in the sense that Christians are called to be optimistic, cheerful types, no matter what difficulties life hands them. The complete phrase is "steadfastness of hope *in our Lord Jesus Christ*" (emphasis added), and we do not have to read far into 1 Thessalonians to know that this is a very particular hope, the hope of Jesus' return or *parousia*. As early as 1:10 Paul specifically characterizes Christians as those who "wait for his Son from heaven," and he returns to this topic again and again (2:19; 3:13; 4:13—5:11; 5:23).

The agenda of the letter, roughly speaking, is now set: the proclamation of the gospel and the Thessalonians' response to that proclamation (1:2—2:16), the continuing concern of Paul and his colleagues for the Thessalonians' response (2:17—3:13), the behavior appropriate to this gospel (4:1–12; 5:12–24), and the promise of Jesus' return and its consequences in the present (4:13—5:11).

As Paul takes up the first of these topics, the Thessalonians' "work of faith," his description of their faith merits sustained attention, both for what it says and for what it does not say. Particularly in some corners of contemporary North American Christianity, individualism dictates that reports about conversion focus on the stories of particular Christians and their changes in attitude or behavior. If reports about conversion do attend to a community of believers rather than to individuals, those reports likely center on concerns about numbers. A church's health is measured in things that may be quantified—numbers on the roll, numbers in the budget, numbers of square feet in the church building. Paul reveals little that can be quantified, yet he says a great deal about what is important.

A Matter of Imitation (v. 6)

Prominent and problematic among Paul's comments about the Thessalonians is that they are imitators, both of the apostles and of the Lord. This is a theme elsewhere in Paul (most notably in 1 Cor. 4:16; 11:1; Phil. 3:17), but interpreters often overlook it, in part because it does not appear in Romans and Galatians, the letters that dominate discussion of Paul's thought (however, see Gal. 4:12). Perhaps the call to imitation also strikes a jarring note because we perceive imitations as "mere" copies of an original or, worse yet, as simple phonies. Those who imitate others are perceived as betraying themselves. One of the sharpest charges raised against a work of literature or art, for example, is that

15

it is imitative of someone else's style. Moreover, that Paul should praise the Thessalonians for imitating him raises issues of self-aggrandizement and patriarchalism. To put the question sharply: Does Paul actually think that believers should make themselves over in his image?

A closer examination may help address this discomfort and reclaim this neglected and misunderstood motif. In the first place, a wide variety of teachers in Paul's day employed personal example and urged their students to conform to those examples (Benjamin Fiore, *The Function of Personal Example in the Socratic and Pastoral Epistles*). Had Paul avoided the use of example and imitation, he might have appeared to his contemporaries as a person who knew himself unfit as a teacher.

In addition, the order "of us and of the Lord" need not suggest that Paul was more concerned with his own status than with that of the Lord. In 2:5, he combines an appeal to the knowledge of Thessalonians and of God, placing the Thessalonians first and God second ("As you know and as God is our witness . . . "). Again in 2:10, Paul claims that "you are witnesses, and God also." In every case, he puts the more powerful party second.

Perhaps it is more important to notice, both here and elsewhere, what sort of imitation Paul commends. The Thessalonians became imitators "of us and of the Lord," he explains, "for in spite of persecution you received the word with joy inspired by the Holy Spirit" (v. 6). If we press this particular instance of imitation closely, it begins to fall apart. How can it be said that Christ "received the word with joy" in spite of persecution? Indeed, it is hard to say how Paul himself became a believer *in spite of persecution.* Neither Paul's own brief autobiographical remarks nor the stories in Acts depict Paul's conversion occurring despite the threat or presence of persecution. What the Thessalonians imitate in the behavior of Paul and Christ must be some more general dynamic of faith or faithfulness in the presence of adversity (see below on 2:14).

Paul's use of the imitation motif in his later letters differs slightly from this passage. In 1 Thessalonians he writes in the indicative, for he is praising a practice in which believers are already engaged. Elsewhere, he writes in the imperative, urging imitation of the apostles and of Christ as a practice to be cultivated. The difference ought not be exaggerated. Even in this letter, Paul is not merely reporting on past events, as if he were writing an account for the daily news. His celebratory recollection of the behavior of the Thessalonians serves to encourage and reinforce similar behavior in the future.

In later letters, as here in 1 Thessalonians, the call for imitation is a general claim about the shape of the Christian life rather than a specific demand that all Christians think and do and say the same things. In 1 Corinthians 4:16, the call for imitation culminates a lengthy section of the letter that begins with the unworldly wisdom of the cross (1:18) and also considers the topsy-turvy nature of apostolic authority (see especially 4:8–13). Similarly, the call to imitation in 1 Corinthians 11:1 does not concern specific behaviors but the general matter of making decisions "for the glory of God" and the upbuilding of the church (10:31–33; see also Phil. 3:17).

In a sense, the motif of imitation does serve to reinforce apostolic authority. Elizabeth Castelli has characterized Paul's comments about imitation as a "discourse of power." By appealing for other believers to imitate himself, Paul implicitly reinforces his own privileges and authority as an apostle and reinscribes the hierarchical power relationship between himself and the congregations he founded (*Imitating Paul: A Discourse of Power,* especially 89–117).

Paul is not writing in the era of the post-Constantinian church, however. The authority Paul invokes for himself is that of the crucified Lord and his persecuted followers. Also, as further study of this particular letter should make evident, Paul's authority coexists with a powerful sense of connection to other believers, a relationship that yields him as vulnerable to them as they are to him. His work depends on their response (1:8); their faithfulness constitutes his confidence before God at the return of Jesus Christ (2:19); his own life depends on their perseverance (3:8).

Neither does the motif of imitation serve as a means of enforcing a uniform set of behaviors. On the contrary, at Corinth Paul employs the motif while at the same time he seeks to respect diverse attitudes toward the eating of meat sacrificed to idols (see 1 Cor. 8:1—11:1). He does not praise the Thessalonians for wearing what Jesus wore or eating what Paul ate. He praises them for embodying in their own setting a response to the gospel that is consistent with Jesus' own faithfulness and with the faith of their teachers.

A key feature of that response is "joy." The Thessalonians "received the word with joy inspired by the Holy Spirit" (v. 6). Here and elsewhere in the New Testament, the claim that the gospel brings joy stands over against views—inside the church and without— that the Christian faith is so serious a matter that it cannot coexist with laughter. Yet Paul himself finds joy because of the Thessalonians (1 Thess. 2:19–20; 3:9; see also Phil. 4:1) and identifies joy as a characteristic of the kingdom.

17

An Example for All (vv. 7–9a)

In verses 7–9a Paul extravagantly assesses the outcome of the Thessalonians' reception of the gospel: they themselves became an example for believers throughout the Greek mainland. The hyperbole Paul employs here effectively reinforces his point. The Thessalonians were an example for "all" believers. Not only Macedonia and Achaia know about the Thessalonians, but "in every place" their faith is known. It is so well established that Christian preachers "have no need to speak about it." People in other territories are already telling the story the Thessalonians told them about what God had done in Jesus Christ.

The temptation to historical speculation becomes powerful in passages such as this one. On the one hand, the rhetorical flourishes here make it difficult to know how to evaluate Paul's assertions either historically or literally, just as it is hard to estimate the size of a crowd when someone reports that "everyone and his grandmother was there." On the other hand, the very existence of the Acts of the Apostles indicates that early Christian communities did tell both stories of Jesus and stories of Jesus' followers, and some would find in this passage an indication that the Thessalonians themselves undertook a mission parallel to that of Paul.

More significant than such concerns, especially for preachers and teachers, is what these comments reveal about Paul's understanding of the transmission of the gospel itself. The Thessalonians may have been recipients of the gospel, but they were by no means merely passive recipients. Even the way in which they received the gospel has itself become a proclamation. To paraphrase Rudolf Bultmann's dictum about Jesus the proclaimer becoming Jesus who is proclaimed, the imitators here become the imitated, the evangelized become the evangelists.

This initial thanksgiving is so focused on the reception of the gospel that the evangelists themselves receive little attention. Paul will take up that question at length in 2:1–12. Even here, however, he makes an intriguing and revealing comment: "just as you know what kind of persons we proved to be among you for your sake" (v. 5). For the sake of the Thessalonians, Paul and Silvanus and Timothy acted in certain, as yet unspecified, ways. In a story about conversion, we anticipate learning how the converts change. We do not anticipate learning that the evangelists themselves change, yet Paul's words are susceptible to that interpretation.

Another detail in this passage suggests something of the relationship between Paul and the Thessalonians, namely, the density of personal pronouns. In the NRSV, that density can best be seen in the statement just examined ("*you* know what kind of persons *we* proved to be among *you* for *your* sake"). The Greek of verses 2–10 seems to weave together these

18

personal pronouns "you" and "we" in a way that verbally reflects the relationship established between Paul and the Thessalonians.

Turning to God (vv. 9b–10)

In verses 9b–10 Paul concludes this reflection on the "welcome" of the Thessalonians and turns to report exactly what is being said about the Thessalonians. As he does so, in verse 9 he draws on traditional Jewish language for repentance and conversion ("you turned to God from idols, to serve a living and true God"). And in verse 10 he uses several expressions that appear unusual when compared with the later letters. These features of verses 9–10 have prompted debate about the origin of this language, but that debate is less significant than what we learn from a close examination of the text itself.

When Paul says that the Thessalonians "turned to God from idols, to serve a living and true God," he is speaking the language of conversion. Although the church has remembered Paul as the virtual prototype of Christian conversion, it is surprising to find how little Paul himself actually uses conversion language. On those rare occasions when he speaks about his own experience, Paul says that he "saw the Lord" (1 Cor. 9:1; 15:8) or that he received a revelation (Gal. 1:11–17). Sometimes he refers to himself and others as having "believed," by which he evidently means the point at which they came to believe the gospel of Jesus Christ (Rom. 13:11). He does employ the language of "turning" in Galatians, where he fears that the Galatians are converting *away from Christ* (Gal. 4:8) and in the exceedingly complex passage of 2 Cor. 3:16.

In the Septuagint, "turning to God" often describes repentance within Israel, as in Deuteronomy 30:2 ("and return to the Lord your God"; see also 1 Sam. 7:3; 1 Kings 8:33; Isa. 6:10; Jer. 24:7; Joel 2:12–14; Zech. 1:3; Sirach 5:7; 17:25). Elsewhere in Jewish literature, however, "turning to God" is used for the conversion of Gentiles to belief in Israel's God. For example, Tobit 14:6 anticipates the time when the nations "will all be converted [lit., "turn"] and worship God in truth." In the New Testament, Luke employs "turning to God" to refer to those Gentiles who come to believe both in Israel's God and in Jesus as the son of that same God (Acts 15:19; 26:18, 20).

The additional description of God as "a living and true God" makes it clear that "turned to God" refers to conversion. Here Paul echoes a well-established Jewish polemic against the religious practices of Gentiles whose gods, from the perspective of Jews, were neither living nor true (see, for example, Isa. 44:9–20; Wisd. Sol. 13–15; Philo, *Decalogue* 52–81; *Special Laws* 1:13–31).

19

This comment about the Thessalonians turning "to God from idols" almost certainly means that Paul is addressing a group that is overwhelmingly Gentile (see Introduction). The discussion of sexual morality in 4:1–8 similarly presupposes that this is a Gentile group in need of instruction. That Luke's story in Acts 17 indicates there were Jewish converts in Thessalonica probably means that Luke has conformed his story about Thessalonica to his customary pattern in narrating the Pauline mission (i.e., Paul routinely begins work in a new city by preaching in a synagogue, only to find his claims rejected by Jews, which forces him to take the gospel among Gentiles).

More important than this demographic point, however, is the assumption underlying Paul's language. In common with Jewish tradition and with emerging Christian tradition, Paul's words about turning *from* idols to serve God imply that faith in the God of Israel who is the Father of Jesus Christ is not an optional practice to be added on to previous values and commitments. One cannot serve this God alongside idols; they must be put away. The claims of Christian faith are all-encompassing.

Central to the gospel the Thessalonians welcomed is the word about God's son, here summarized in verse 10. As noted earlier, several elements in this verse are anomalous: (1) Although the NRSV obscures the distinction, here Paul refers to Jesus coming "from heavens," rather than "from heaven," as is his habit in later letters (see, e.g., Rom. 1:18; 1 Cor. 15:47; 2 Cor. 5:2; Gal. 1:18). (2) Rather than speaking of resurrection "from *the* dead," as here, Paul prefers to omit the article ("from dead"), as in Rom. 1:4; 1 Cor. 15:12–13, 20; Gal. 1:2; Phil. 3:11. (These distinctions will not be evident in the NRSV.) (3) Most important, Paul seldom uses the designation "Jesus" without the addition of "Christ" or "Lord." (4) The logic of the verse also presents a question: Why does Paul identify the son as being in heaven and then apparently backtrack to refer to Jesus' resurrection from the dead? (5) Familiarity with Paul's later letters also prompts readers to notice that nothing is said here of the cross, which he later identifies as the content of Christian preaching (see especially 1 Cor. 1:18; 2:2; Gal. 3:1).

Some scholars explain these anomalies in verses 9–10 by theorizing that Paul is quoting from, and perhaps modifying, a Jewish-Christian formula about the conversion of Gentiles. The similarities between these verses and language attributed to early Christian preaching in Acts lends support to such a notion. If Paul is indeed drawing on already established traditions, then here he offers a glimpse of very early Christian reflection on the person and work of Jesus.

20

There are problems with such theories. As noted above, the language about "turning to God" is conventional in Jewish literature and need not be Jewish-Christian as such. Also, if 1 Thessalonians is Paul's earliest letter, then arguing that an expression is not "Pauline" becomes extremely precarious.

Whatever the history of verses 9–10 and whatever the difficulties with reconciling elements of this passage with the later Pauline letters, it does contain major themes of 1 Thessalonians—the turning of these particular Gentiles to the service of God (and the implications of that turning) and the expectation of Jesus' return (and the implications of that return).

The passage concludes with the identification of Jesus as the one "who rescues us from the wrath that is coming." Although verse 10 does not identify this wrath with God, later Paul makes it clear that this is not an impersonal wrath or the wrath of a superhuman being but is God's own wrath, God's righteous response to persistent, implacable human disobedience (2:16). The image is familiar from the Old Testament, where wrath is a feature of the day of the Lord, the day of judgment (see, e.g., Isa. 13:6–19). As will be the case in Paul's references to God's wrath in Romans (1:18; 2:5, 8; 3:5; 5:9; 9:22), here God's wrath is not something that should terrify believers, for they may trust in the one who rescues them from that wrath (see especially 1 Thess. 5:9).

The urgency and the tension in this verse should not be over-looked. The "wrath" is coming. Although Paul says nothing about when this day of judgment will arrive, he will later warn about its suddenness and inevitability (see 5:1–5). Similarly, Jesus is—even now, in the present—rescuing from that wrath.

The temptation with texts of this sort is either to dismiss them as remnants of a worldview now passé or to insist that all Christians must affirm each word in every apocalyptic scene in literalistic fashion. Either dismissing or reifying this passage and others like it permits us to escape momentarily the uncomfortable notion that we are in need of deliverance. Perhaps as disruptive to modern sensibilities as the notion that God is wrathful is the confession that human beings require rescue from that wrath. Particularly in the context of North American Christianity, which has elevated self-reliance and independence to a Christian virtue, the admission that Christians—indeed, even faithful Christians who serve as examples to others—need deliverance borders on the shocking.

In verses 9–10, Paul employs three verbs to describe the experience of the Thessalonians: turn, serve, and wait. As already explained, the first verb is that of the conversion itself. The second, "serve" (Gr. *douleuein*) would be better translated as "serve as slaves" or "be enslaved to," for the verb derives from the noun "slave." However wholly opposed such language is to our society's intense sense of autonomy, it

21

recognizes frankly that human beings do not choose to do God's will; they do it because they are called, because they are under orders. That compulsion in turn brings with it an extraordinary joy and even freedom, but it is first of all compulsion.

The last verb, "wait," may sound downright peculiar, particularly to Western ears attuned to the language of pragmatism and activism. Those who "wait around" for something to happen merit little sympathy and less praise. For Paul, however, to wait is to expect. To wait is also to acknowledge that something is out of our hands. Here he anticipates 5:1–11 with its reminder that the timetable for Jesus' return belongs to God and God alone. Waiting for God, in this sense, is a prime attribute of the Christian life.

Careful attention to the experience of the Thessalonians in turning, serving, and waiting should not prevent noticing that it is God who makes the experience of the Thessalonians possible. Paul's thanksgiving begins by thanking God for the Thessalonians, not the Thessalonians for their acknowledgment of God (v. 2). One temptation in preaching this text, particularly because the lectionary introduces it during what will be stewardship season in many congregations, is to thank the congregation for all that they are doing for God's sake. But it is God who chose and loved the Thessalonians (v. 4), and the Holy Spirit which made the gospel manifest among them (v. 5) and filled them with joy (v. 6). The "word of the Lord" sounds forth (v. 8). It is God who raised Jesus from the dead, and God's son who is Savior (v. 10). Paul does not argue these claims. He assumes them and recalls them only briefly, but that does not license overlooking them. The "welcome" given Paul and his coworkers is more than a welcome to human beings; it is a welcome to God (v. 9, see especially 2:13).

Remembering the Work of the Apostles

1 THESSALONIANS 2:1–16

With the opening of chapter 2, Paul adjusts the lens through which he examines events in Thessalonica. In 1:2–10 he has focused on the experience of the Thessalonians, placing himself and his coworkers well

22

in the background. Here, in 2:1–16, Paul's behavior and that of his coworkers comes to the foreground.

Following the transition (vv. 1–2) this recollection of the visit of the apostles to Thessalonica begins with a series of negative assertions (vv. 3–7a). Here Paul denies that the apostles were guilty of a variety of self-aggrandizing behaviors, including deceit, trickery, flattery, and greed. In verse 7b he turns to a series of positive assertions with which he characterizes the apostles' visit. Verses 13–16 return to thanksgiving for the manner in which the Thessalonians responded to the activity of the apostles, concluding with an enormously problematic comment about the responsibility of "the Jews" for Jesus' death.

1 Thessalonians 2:1–12
Apostles
Worthy of God

Whatever the circumstances under which Paul and his coworkers arrived in Thessalonica, they must not have been promising. The NRSV reports that they had "already suffered and been shamefully mistreated at Philippi," although the Greek *hybrizein* might be rendered by "insulted" or "scoffed at" rather than by the harsher language of "shamefully mistreated." This harsher translation of the NRSV almost certainly takes its cues from Luke's story of Paul and Silas's imprisonment in Philippi (Acts 16:16–40). Without that narrative, interpreters might be less inclined to imagine that the apostles had been the recipients of physical abuse in Philippi, particularly since Paul's letter to the Philippians makes no reference to mistreatment in that city.

Whatever the circumstances that surrounded it, Paul recalls that "our coming to you was not in vain" (v. 1). The expression "not in vain" is an instance of litotes, a figure of speech in which something is emphasized by negating its opposite. The same rhetorical strategy is at work in Romans 1:16, "For I am not ashamed of the gospel," as well as in the contemporary colloquialism, "His new Mercedes is not too shabby!" The confidence expressed here stands in tension with the anxiety revealed in 3:5 (see below on 2:17—3:5).

Verse 2 amplifies this claim about the initial visit: "we had courage in our God to declare to you the gospel of God in spite of great opposition." What normally passes for common sense might have dictated

23

that Paul and his companions enter Thessalonica with caution. The difficulties they encountered in Philippi, whatever they were, could have caused Paul and his companions to consider a more modest approach in the next city. Yet Paul insists that the opposite happened; rather than seeking more diplomatic strategies, the apostles were encouraged. To have courage or, better, to be emboldened (Gr. *parrhēsiazomai*) was a trait highly prized in a philosophical teacher. In those cases, however, the philosopher carefully determines whether the circumstances favor bold or frank speech. Plutarch's essay *How to Tell a Flatterer from a Friend* addresses this issue at length (especially paragraphs 66E— 74E). He warns against confusing frankness with abusive speech or mere faultfinding. The one who speaks out must consider the time and the situation, so that the speaker instructs but does not humiliate. In other words, the friend should be shrewd enough to know when to speak forthrightly and when to be silent.

Paul contradicts this ideal regarding frankness or boldness in two ways. First, his boldness is not a personal characteristic or an achievement based on wisdom or education. It derives from God ("we had courage in our God"). Although the Greek is a bit ambiguous here, it probably means that Paul and his colleagues are empowered by God. Verse 4 makes his claim more explicit: they were approved by God to be entrusted with the gospel.

Second, Paul is bold despite circumstances that might have warranted silence ("in spite of great opposition"). Paul never explains the nature of this "great opposition," presumably because the recipients of the letter know what has occurred. Those who read the letter alongside the stories of Acts will readily think of opposition from Jews and the attack on Jason (Acts 17:1–9). The word *agōn*, which the NRSV translates as "opposition," literally refers to an athletic contest, and figuratively to a public debate. What Paul refers to, then, may well be the ridicule to which traveling moral philosophers were routinely subjected. Regardless of the circumstances, Paul and his colleagues spoke with courage or boldness.

Paul uses this expression similarly in later letters. In 2 Corinthians 3:12 it refers to the freedom and confidence of the apostles in proclaiming the gospel and in 2 Corinthians 7:4 to his direct speech concerning the Corinthians (see also Phil. 1:20 and Philemon 8). This notion of bold or frank speech also plays an interesting role in Acts, when the Jerusalem community prays for boldness in the face of persecution (4:29, 31). For Luke, bold speech is a sign of the church's witness to the resurrected Lord (see, e.g., 4:13; 9:27–28; 13:46; 28:31; see also Heb. 3:6; 4:16; 10:19, 35; 1 John 2:28; 3:32; 4:17; 5:14).

Not from Deceit (vv. 3–7a)

Following this initial characterization of the visit, the negative assertions of verses 3–7a raise a pressing question about how this passage ought to be read. If a contemporary minister should stand before her congregation on Sunday morning and announce, "I have not acted out of deceit or trickery or greed," the immediate response of those present would be to wonder what charges had been raised against the pastor, by whom, and on what evidence. The announcement of the minister would almost certainly be heard as an act of self-defense, particularly in a North American context that thrives on scandals in the lives of public figures.

One approach to this passage is to read it in just that way, as an act of self-defense. Paul (and perhaps his coworkers as well) has been charged with gross improprieties, and this is his apology for his behavior.

Two considerations make that approach to the passage difficult, one internal to the letter and one external. First, the letter does not otherwise suggest that Paul felt himself to be on the defensive with the Thessalonians. Second, Abraham J. Malherbe has shown features of this passage to be common fare among philosophers who wished to distinguish themselves from disreputable figures who presented themselves to the public as teachers (" 'Gentle as a Nurse': The Cynic Background to I Thess ii"). For example, Dio Chrysostom, a Stoic philosopher active late in the first century, complains that

> to find a man who in plain terms and without guile speaks his mind with frankness, and neither for the sake of reputation nor for gain makes false pretensions, but out of good will and concern for his fellow-men stands ready, if need be, to submit to ridicule and to the disorder and the uproar of the mob—to find such a man as that is not easy.
>
> (*Discourse* 32.11)

Both Paul and Dio Chrysostom deny that their motivation stems from self-interest or self-aggrandizement. Both speak with frankness. Both are prepared to endure the scorn of others in order to tell the truth. They will not be swayed by something as evanescent as a crowd's approval or disapproval. Much that Paul says here, then, is conventional in the self-description of a serious philosopher and need not suggest that Paul seeks to respond to charges made against him.

The goals and convictions that undergird Paul's remarks, however, would not have been shared by the conventional Hellenistic philosopher. Although Dio Chrysostom asserts in passing that he believes he has been chosen for his vocation "by the will of some deity" (*Discourse* 32.12), little else suggests that he perceives himself to be governed or instructed

25

by a deity. By contrast, Paul affirms that he has been "approved by God to be entrusted with the message of the gospel." Dio works for the general betterment of the populace; such enhancement is, for Paul, only a by-product of his fundamental task of pleasing God (v. 4).

The negative claims of verses 3–7a conclude with the reminder "though we might have made demands as apostles of Christ." The Greek idiom at work here literally means "we were able to be weighty." It resembles the contemporary colloquialism that designates someone important as a "heavy" (e.g., the "heavy hitters"). Exactly how the apostles might be "heavies" Paul leaves unstated, but the fact that a related verb appears in verse 9 suggests that the demands might be financial. The apostles were not greedy, although they might have asked for support.

Later letters may be helpful in teasing out the implications here. First Corinthians 9:3–14 asserts that apostles have a right to be supported financially. The line Paul walks in these matters is a fine one. Sometimes, as here in 1 Thessalonians, he insists that he has not taken money from believers so that no one can say he has taken advantage of them (as in 1 Cor. 9:12b, 15; see also 2 Cor. 12:14). Yet he regards it as important to acknowledge the principle that the apostles merit support, and some will later criticize him for *not* taking money (2 Cor. 12:13).

The utter familiarity of the term "apostles" makes it easy to overlook, but this is the first time the word appears in this letter and therefore the first evidence of its use in Christian circles. What makes this instance particularly intriguing is that the plural surely includes Timothy and Silvanus, people who are not customarily identified with the apostles. For Paul, unlike Luke, that office is not limited to twelve and restricted to those who witnessed Jesus' ministry (see Acts 1:13, 15–26, although he does link his own calling with seeing the risen Lord, as in 1 Cor. 9:1; 15:8). Paul implicitly defines an apostle as one commissioned by God for the particular task of proclaiming the gospel of Jesus Christ (see, for example, Rom. 1:1; 1 Cor. 1:1), one whose vocation is evident from the response of others to the gospel (1 Cor. 9:1–2).

Tender Nurture (vv. 7b–8)

Following the introduction of "apostles of Christ," the positive assertions begin, and the first among them has generated considerable controversy. As the footnote to verse 7 in the NRSV indicates, some early manuscripts read "we were infants among you," instead of the NRSV's "we were gentle." The difference between the Greek words for "infants" (Gr. *nēpioi*) and "gentle" (Gr. *ēpioi*) consists of a single letter so that a scribe might easily confuse the two words. Scholars are divided on this question, and while it may appear to be a technical matter of interest only to specialists, it becomes important in light of the use of familial imagery throughout the passage (see below).

The evidence in ancient manuscripts favors "infants," but many scholars insist on "gentle" because of the difficulty of understanding what it would mean to say that "we were infants among you, like a nurse tenderly caring for her own children." On the other hand, one principle used in deciding between conflicting readings in early manuscripts is that the more difficult reading (one that is awkward grammatically or theologically) is likely to be the earlier or more original reading since scribes would be more inclined to correct problems than to introduce them. (For example, a few manuscripts read "Joseph and his mother," in Luke 2:43 instead of "his parents." According to the principle of the more difficult reading, "his parents" is probably earlier because it is more difficult theologically than "Joseph and his mother." The alteration presumably occurred because a scribe feared that readers would understand Joseph to be Jesus' biological father.) In addition, Paul certainly makes abrupt shifts of imagery in other passages (see, e.g., Gal. 4:19). It is also noteworthy that he describes the apostles as "orphans" in 2:17. It may well be, then, that Paul wrote "infants" rather than "gentle." That is, the apostles were not "heavies," making much of themselves through various demands (v. 7a), but were as unassuming among the Thessalonians as infants.

With the end of verse 7, Paul introduces a highly evocative image for the apostles, that of the "nurse tenderly caring for her own children." The use of nurses, wet nurses, or lactating nurses in particular, was widespread in the Greco-Roman world. Physicians sometimes advised mothers against breast-feeding their own children and provided advice on the selection of wet nurses. Nor were wet nurses used only for the children of wealthy families. As Keith R. Bradley has shown ("Wet-Nursing at Rome: A Study in Social Relations"), it was not unusual for slave infants to have wet nurses, either because the mother had died in childbirth or because the mother and infant had been separated by property transfer. Some householders would also employ a wet nurse rather than forego the work of the slave mother. The nurse was not only a common but a beloved figure, as is clear in literary references and from the number of inscriptions in which adults honor those who nursed them.

To compare the apostles, then, with the nurse, is to invoke an image of loving concern. Paul multiplies this image by specifying that the nurse is "caring for her own children." However warm the connection between the nurse and her charges, children of another woman, that

27

between the nurse and her own children would be even more intense. Verse 8 serves to unpack what is implicit in the nurse metaphor: the apostles regard the Thessalonians as so dear that they share with them their very selves.

What makes this image most astonishing, of course, is the fact that Paul applies it to himself and his coworkers. Some male writers in Paul's day, such as Dio Chrysostom, do refer to the particular care given an infant by a nurse, but they do so in quite negative terms (e.g., adults should outgrow the need for a nurse). More important, such writers employ the nurse as an example to illustrate another point, not as a metaphor to describe themselves. They do not number *themselves* among the wet nurses.

One exception that may well have influenced Paul comes not from a contemporary but from hundreds of years earlier in the Old Testament. Moses complains to God,

> Did I conceive all this people? Did I give birth to them, that you should say to me, "Carry them in your bosom, as a nurse carries a sucking child," to the land that you promised on oath to their ancestors?
> (Num. 11:12)

Although Moses laments the role in which he finds himself, he nevertheless recognizes that he is now nurse—like it or not—to Israel, and he applies that term to himself. (For further discussion see Gaventa, "Apostles as Babes and Nurses"; and "Reflection: Maternal Imagery in Paul," pp. 31–34 below.)

Apostles Worthy of God
(vv. 9–12)

Again in verse 9, Paul prefaces a specific recollection with "you remember," calling attention to the importance of what follows. The apostles worked among the Thessalonians, not just from morning to night, but "night and day." Such claims about the apostles' labor seem slightly out of place in this discussion of their integrity and affection, especially if some among the Thessalonians regarded manual labor with scorn or contempt (see below on 4:9–12). Perhaps Paul introduces them by way of anticipating his own admonitions to the Thessalonians in 4:11–12 and 5:12–14. Here he offers the apostles' behavior as a model for others.

28   In the conclusion of the passage, Paul takes up yet another image for the apostles' relationship with the Thessalonians, that of the father with his children. Elsewhere, Paul speaks of himself as a father in the

sense that he metaphorically begets believers; that is, the comparison is restricted to the initial time of conversion (Philemon 10; 1 Cor. 4:15). Although here also he is discussing his initial encounter with the Thessalonians, he extends the image to include his initial instruction and exhortation.

The conclusion of the passage also makes it clear that the relationship between God and the Thessalonians involves all of life. Paul knows no distinction between believing and doing. He urges the Thessalonians to "lead a life worthy of God, who calls you into his own kingdom and glory." The lineaments of that life, or some of them, come into play later in the letter (4:1–12, 5:6–22). Here it suffices to notice that believers live worthily of the God who calls them. That is, they do not live in order to get God to call them or accept them, but to be consistent with the very goodness of God.

Perhaps the most striking feature of the assertions in verses 7b–12 is the way in which they invoke a variety of familial relations. The apostles were infants, they were nurse-mothers, and they were fathers. Just a little later, Paul will claim that the separation from the Thessalonians rendered the apostles orphans (3:17). Throughout the letter, he addresses the Thessalonians as "brothers and sisters" (the Greek has only "brothers"). Consistent with this use of familial language is the highly affective character of Paul's description of the relationship between apostles and converts.

From a sociological perspective, the use of familial language is not surprising. Wayne Meeks has noted the extensive use of familial imagery in Paul's letters and has argued that it serves to reinforce the boundary lines around the community (*The First Urban Christians*, 85–88). Particularly for those Christians who may have experienced severe conflict with family and neighbors over their new convictions, even the loss of family in some instances, family language serves to create a new family in place of the old.

If the presence of familial imagery does not itself surprise us, the frequency with which Paul changes images does. In this passage, the apostles begin as infants, they transform into mothers, then in another moment they become fathers, and finally they are orphans. Perhaps this array confirms what Paul insists, namely, that the Thessalonians became "very dear," so that only multiple, even bewildering, images capture the multiple layers of connection. The frequently changing imagery may also subvert the popular notion that Paul takes a thoroughly hierarchical stance toward the churches. Particularly in a society with highly structured perceptions of maleness and femaleness, a man who speaks of himself as an infant or as a nurse-mother or as an orphan voluntarily hands over his place in the conventional gender hierarchy, however fleetingly.

The tender, moving tones with which Paul speaks of the apostles' relationship with the Thessalonians should not obscure the fact that this is not only a social relationship, but one with profoundly theocentric origins. Three times in this brief passage Paul depicts the apostles' activity in terms of "the gospel of God." They declared the gospel (v. 2), shared it (v. 8), and proclaimed it (v. 9). What makes the phrase "the gospel of God" more striking is that Paul employs it only three other times in all his later letters (Rom. 1:1; 15:16; 2 Cor. 11:7); and its use in verse 9 in connection with "proclaim" (Gr. *kēryssein*) matches exactly Mark's depiction of the initial ministry of Jesus, who "came to Galilee, proclaiming the good news [the gospel] of God" (Mark 1:14). This parallel suggests that the formulation may be an early one. What the apostles declare, then, is God's own good news. Because of their location in God (v. 2), they speak this gospel boldly. They do so with the sole desire of pleasing God (v. 4).

This passage, where Paul appears to be working out his own understanding of apostleship, offers important clues about the nature of Christian ministry. Too often when we turn to the Bible in connection with questions of ministry, we linger over texts that emphasize the power or authority of those individuals who are commissioned. Here, by contrast, those who are "entrusted with the message of the gospel" know that the gospel is not their own possession (despite the wording of 1:5). They work, not for their own promotion, but on behalf of that gospel. They do not pass along the gospel as if it were a commodity that might be packaged and conveyed from hand to hand without altering the ones who pass it on; instead, they are themselves involved in this passing along, so that they are vulnerable and involved and profoundly connected.

A story that makes a poignant illustration of this relationship appears in later Jewish tradition, which preserves a number of stories about the giving of the Torah to Israel. One of them compares God's gift of the Torah with a king who gives his daughter in marriage to another king. The father insists that there must always be a room for himself in the house of his daughter and her new husband, because he cannot be parted from her. The story concludes, "With the Torah you, as it were, take also me." If the social assumptions in the anecdote collide with the feminist sensibilities of contemporary hearers, the analogy is nevertheless clear: Torah is God's own; God cannot be parted from Torah. In a limited sense, what Paul says about apostolic ministry in this passage resembles the rabbinic story. Apostles cannot give over the gospel without also giving over something of themselves.

To read this passage as if it addressed only apostles or only ordained ministers, however, would be mistaken. If this text is paraenetic,
that is, if it is instructive for the Thessalonians rather than merely recalling their past or defending Paul and his colleagues, then it addresses
all Christians. It raises questions about who is being pleased by the way
in which we live and the choices we make. And it makes unsettling suggestions about the kinds of relationships that should characterize Christian life.

This passage also provides an interesting place for reflecting on the
way in which we read the Bible. Many who espouse a high view of biblical authority and wish to read the Bible as a pattern for the church's
life might find difficulty with 2:9. If Paul worked "night and day" so as
not to require support ("burden") the Thessalonians, that might require
that all clergy should have "tent-making" ministries; they should support themselves in secular employment so that their churches will not
have the burden of their salaries. Although tent-making ministries have
much to offer in some settings, they also pose difficulties for many others. Because we have no intention of requiring tent-making ministry,
we do not hesitate to read "around" this verse.

This passage also offers an occasion for reflecting on the various
ways in which the church fits in with, or stands over against, or borrows
from culture. Here Paul borrows the language of the culture (philosophical schools) but affirms that he pleases not mortals but God. While
various voices in the church advocate a firm stand against culture and
others seem to baptize anything affirmed by the larger society, at least
one model we find in scripture is far more subtle. Paul employs the language of his day, but he does so in ways that are determined to speak
the gospel, not the culture's presuppositions.

REFLECTION:
Maternal Imagery in the Letters of Paul

Paul's characterization of the apostolic role in the first two chapters of 1 Thessalonians ranks among the most moving passages of his
letters. The Thessalonians are "very dear" to Paul and his coworkers.
He employs intimate family terms to capture that sense of closeness.
Among those expressions, as we have already seen in the commentary,   31
one that stands out occurs in 2:7: "[We were among you] like a nurse
tenderly caring for her own children."

Paul does not use this precise expression again, but he does employ maternal imagery in several letters. In some cases, as here in 1 Thess. 2:7, he speaks of himself in frankly maternal terms. Perhaps the most fascinating of these texts is Gal. 4:19: "My little children, for whom I am again in the pain of childbirth until Christ is formed in you."

The logic of Galatians 4:19 intrigues as well as perplexes. Paul is the mother of believers in the Galatian churches. He is in the process of giving birth to them *again*. Whatever the circumstance in those churches, he views it a threat so powerful that he can think of this as a second labor. Paul remains in labor, not until the child is born, but until Christ is formed in the child (see Gaventa, "The Maternity of Paul").

Again in Romans 8:22, Paul draws on the vocabulary of childbirth: "the whole creation has been groaning in labor pains until now; and not only the creation, but we ourselves, who have the first fruits of the Spirit, groan inwardly while we wait for our adoption, the redemption of our bodies." Unlike Galatians 4:19, this passage does not comment on the apostolic role; rather, it gives expression to Paul's deep convictions about the hope of believers. In common with Galatians 4:19, however, Paul makes torturous logical steps as he moves from the labor groans of creation to that of believers, who then groan for their adoption rather than for the giving of birth.

Another passage, in 1 Corinthians 3, does find Paul drawing on maternal imagery for his work. Here he chides the Corinthians for their immature behavior: "I could not speak to you as spiritual people, but rather as people of the flesh, as infants in Christ. I fed you with milk, not solid food, for you were not ready for solid food." To populations who take for granted the baby bottle and infant formula, the maternal imagery here may be elusive. In Paul's world, however, only the mother or the wet nurse can supply an infant with milk.

In two other passages, maternal imagery concerns Paul's own birth, both a literal and a figurative birth. Galatians 1:15 echoes the prophetic calls of Isaiah 49:1–6 and Jeremiah 1:5 when Paul asserts that God "had set me apart before I was born. . . . " And in 1 Cor. 15:8, Paul refers to himself as "one untimely born." This phrase translates a rare Greek word the precise nuance of which in context is disputed, but Paul does here identify his apostleship by means of birth imagery.

Many readers of the New Testament find the existence of these passages startling. Because our expectations shape much of what we see in texts, these passages largely fall outside our reading "radar." That was 32 not the case with our predecessors in the Christian faith. Included among the prayers of Anselm, for example, is an extended prayer to Paul which addresses Paul as "the nurse of the faithful, caressing his sons" (*The Prayers and Meditations of Saint Anselm,* 152). Until very recently, however, the scholarly literature has paid little or no attention to these passages, often explicitly categorizing them as instances of Paul's use of *paternal* imagery (see Gaventa, "Our Mother St. Paul").

Maternal and paternal imagery are not the same, however, and Paul does not use the two interchangeably. When Paul speaks in unambiguously paternal language, he does so with reference to the origin of faith in the life of a person or group (as in 1 Cor. 4:15; 1 Thess. 2:11; Philemon 10). Maternal imagery serves a different function, one more concerned with the nurture and growth of believers than with the point at which they were called into faith.

In addition, unlike instances of paternal imagery, several of the passages in which Paul employs maternal imagery reflect Paul's apocalyptic viewpoint. The language of birth pangs frequently appears in biblical writings that anticipate the arrival of the day of the Lord and the turmoil that will precede that age. Isaiah, for example, warns,

> Wail, for the day of the Lord is near;
> it will come like destruction from the Almighty!
> Pangs and agony will seize them;
> they will be in anguish like a woman in labor.
> They will look aghast at one another;
> their faces will be aflame.
> (Isa. 13:6, 8)

Other instances of this use of maternal imagery in the context of apocalyptic appear in Micah 4:10; Jeremiah 6:24; Mark 13:8; and Revelation 12:2.

The very fact of maternal imagery in Paul's letters is fascinating, but the question inevitably comes: What does it mean to find Paul, whom George Bernard Shaw termed the "eternal enemy" of women, using language that belongs to the world of mothers and their children? This question cries out for more research and reflection, but several possibilities include the following:

First, as noted earlier in discussion of this passage, Paul's use of maternal language is another way of cultivating a family relationship among Christians. To be a child of the apostle is to be closely connected to him and to others who are also "children" of the apostle. Believers belong to the same family.

Second, when Paul speaks of himself as a mother, he makes himself vulnerable. A woman who is in labor with a child knows that she is vulnerable; she is not in control of how her labor will progress or when the child will actually appear. A nursing mother is also vulnerable, for babies set their own feeding schedules, to which mothers necessarily conform.

Third, in the Greco-Roman world of the first century, mothers do not have the same authority as fathers, the heads of households. When Paul presents himself as a mother, he voluntarily hands over the authority of a patriarch and identifies himself with the subordinate role of the female in a society where female-identified males were subject to ridicule. That should not be surprising from one who elsewhere refers to the apostles as "last of all" (1 Cor. 4:9), "the rubbish of the world, the dregs of all things" (1 Cor. 4:13).

1 Thessalonians 2:13–16
Receiving and Opposing the Word of God

Paul returns now to the task of giving thanks for the Thessalonians. This second thanksgiving constitutes a departure from conventional letter form, an anomaly that has prompted suggestions that an early editor inserted a fragment from a second letter here. (More serious questions are raised about the authenticity of vv. 14–16, on which see below.) Many elements in these verses closely parallel earlier statements in the letter's opening lines, making it more likely that 2:13 serves to repeat and make emphatic the thanksgiving begun in 1:2. God is the one to be thanked (2:13 and 1:2). The Thessalonians received the gospel (2:13 and 1:5). God is at work among them (2:13 and 1:4). The Thessalonians have become imitators of other believers (2:14 and 1:6). Paul's desire for upbuilding, for consolidating the faith of the Thessalonians, issues forth in this repetition of thanks to God and praise of the Thessalonians.

Verse 13 warrants close attention. The NRSV nicely captures the difference between the two actions of the Thessalonians in welcoming the gospel: "when you received the word of God . . . you accepted it." Elsewhere "receive" (Gr. paralambanein) has the connotation of active acceptance (as in 1 Cor. 15:2 of the acceptance of traditions about the resurrection), but here there seems to be a slight emphasis on the second action. In colloquial English, we might say that the Thessalonians not only "took" the gospel but also "took to it."

The significant contrast in the verse depends less on the verbs, however, than it does on the play between "word of God" and "human word." In the Greek, these phrases stand in sharp opposition as "word of humans" and "word of God." Particularly in light of the extended dis-

34

cussion of the apostles' conduct in 2:1–12, it is important to notice that what the Thessalonians received was not the apostles' word but God's. This recalls the repetition of "gospel of God" in verses 2, 8, and 9. Paul takes no chance on confusion over this point.

In addition, God's word is now "at work in you believers." Whatever the importance of the apostles and their labor, God is now active among the Thessalonians themselves. The apostles have been and will continue to be significant for them, but it is also the case that God works among them directly, just as God chose them in the beginning (1:4).

A Non-Pauline Fragment? (vv. 14–16)

As Paul explains exactly how the Thessalonians have become imitators, he draws a puzzling parallel. The Thessalonians imitate the churches in Judea, "for you suffered the same things from your own compatriots as they did from the Jews" (v. 14). The explanation in verses 15–16 of what "the Jews" did presents interpreters with serious problems. First, it seems out of place here. Reference to the Jews interrupts Paul's recollection about his relationship with the Thessalonians. In fact, one could skip from the end of verse 13 to the beginning of verse 17 and not sense that something had been omitted. The reference also seems out of place in that this letter addresses a predominantly Gentile congregation, one with little knowledge of Jewish tradition or history.

Second, Paul does not elsewhere claim that the Jews killed Jesus. This statement would be more at home in the Acts of the Apostles, where Jesus' death is attributed to the ignorance and malice of Jerusalem Jews (Acts 2:23; 3:14–15; 13:27–28) or in Matthew's Gospel, where Jews explicitly take upon themselves responsibility for Jesus' death (Matt. 27:25). Only in 1 Corinthians 2:6 might Paul be understood as assigning human responsibility for Jesus' death, when he recalls that "powers of this age" put Jesus to death, although these are probably cosmic rather than human rulers. Elsewhere, Paul ascribes Jesus' death to his own self-giving (see, for example, Gal. 1:4; 2:19; Phil. 2:8) or to God's will (see Gal. 1:4; Rom. 3:25).

Third, the assertion that Jews "displease God and oppose everyone" sounds suspiciously like well-known *Gentile* slurs against Jews. For example, the Jewish historian Josephus, a contemporary of Paul, reports on Gentile claims that Jews swear oaths before God to oppose all foreigners (*Contra Apion* 2.121). Similar comments about Jewish hatred of non-Jews appear in works of the Roman satirist Juvenal (*Satire*

35

14.103.4) and in the historian Tacitus (*Histories* 5.5.2). What Paul says, then, might reflect conventional Gentile slander regarding Jews, but that does not explain what such comments are doing here, on the lips of a Jew. Even if we classify them as prophetic outrage, the strident language we would expect from an Amos or an Isaiah, it is hard to hear Paul address such stinging words *about* Jews to a Gentile audience. These are the sorts of things one says to siblings at home, not in public beyond the confines of the family.

Finally, however it is translated, the announcement about God's wrath is difficult to reconcile with the extended discussion of Israel Paul produces in Romans 9—11. There, as he struggles to articulate the apparent contradiction between God's election of Israel and the refusal of most Jews to confess Jesus as the Christ of Israel, Paul says none of the ugly things affirmed here. By striking contrast, he concludes that reflection with the claim that "all Israel will be saved," a claim that stands in tension with 2:16.

Recognizing these substantial problems, some scholars have argued that verses 14–16 are an interpolation, added later by a scribe, almost certainly a Gentile Christian at home in the world of anti-Jewish sentiment. In a particular current event, perhaps the destruction of the Jerusalem Temple by the Romans in 70 C.E., this individual sees a sign of divine judgment against Jews for their rejection of the gospel.

Attractive as such a solution might be, it lacks any solid support in the text. No manuscript of 1 Thessalonians omits these lines or transposes them to another place (by contrast with other disputed passages, such as 1 Cor. 14:34–35, which appears in some manuscripts following verse 40 rather than verse 33, or the well-known story of the woman taken in adultery, which some manuscripts place after John 7 and others after John 21:25 or Luke 21:38). In addition, the introduction to verse 14 ("For you, brothers and sisters") anticipates and parallels the introduction to verse 17 ("As for us, brothers and sisters").

The better question, then, is how to understand the passage in its context. The date of the letter may play a crucial role in interpreting these difficult lines. This letter does not discuss the cross and its significance as do the later letters, which makes it difficult to assess the state of Paul's reflection on Jesus' death. His comments here may have much in common with statements in the Gospels and Acts precisely because he has heard them from others who preceded him in the faith.

Another possibility is that Paul has in mind here "the Judeans" rather than "the Jews" (the Greek word can be translated either way). That is, he is speaking of residents of the province of Judea rather than of all Jews. Judeans makes sense of the context, in which the comparison is between the Thessalonians and their compatriots, on the one hand, and believers in Judea and their compatriots, on the other. In other words, the problem is one between neighbors. In any case, of course, he does not have all Jews in mind, since he himself is a Jew and knows other believers who are Jews.

Verse 16a is crucial. Whatever the circumstances and motivation, if groups of Jews interfered with Paul's proclamation of the gospel among the Gentiles, he is likely to have become enraged because he understood that proclamation to be the direct result of God's own will (see, for example, Gal. 1:15). Luke tells so many stories about Jewish resistance, and they resemble one another so closely, that readers need to be skeptical about assuming Jewish resistance occurred just as Luke describes it. Nevertheless, the Pauline letters themselves refer to Jewish resistance (see 2 Cor. 11:24–26, for example). What he writes in 2:14–16, then, may be born out of indignation and frustration, perhaps even a measure of bewilderment that fellow Jews do not share his own convictions.

Admittedly, the language is harsh, but it is a harshness familiar to readers of the Old Testament, and some of the precise charges Paul makes have antecedents there. For example, 1 Chronicles 36:16 reports that the people of Jerusalem "kept mocking the messengers of God, despising his words, and scoffing at his prophets, until the wrath of the Lord against his people became so great that there was no remedy" (see also Matt. 23:29–36 and Luke 11:47–52). Daniel anticipates the end of the rule of the four kingdoms, "when the transgressions have reached their full measure" (8:23; see also 2 Macc. 6:14; Wisd. Sol. 19:3–5). In other words, Paul's polemic borrows heavily on conventional language with which Jews express their outrage at the faithlessness of other Jews.

Translation of verse 16b is notoriously difficult, because the phrase the NRSV gives as "at last" can be translated in a variety of ways. As the NRSV note indicates, "at last" (Gr. *eis telos*) may also be translated "completely" or "forever." Another possibility, although less frequently raised, is that *eis telos* means "until the end" (as in John 13:1). Deciding among these options is difficult because Paul does not elsewhere use this precise combination of preposition and noun. Given the historical character of the preceding description, *eis telos* may well mean "at last" in the sense that God's wrath is finally visible. Reading the text in light of Romans 11:26, on the other hand, would suggest that "until the end" is the better translation. God's wrath will prove to be salvific.

Paul gives no hint whether he finds a particular event to be evidence of God's wrath. Suggestions range from famine in Jerusalem to the expulsion of Jews from Rome under the rule of the emperor

37

Claudius, but it is not clear that any such public event is, for Paul, God's "wrath." He may have perceived the rejection of the gospel itself as wrathful, just as later in Romans he sees God's wrath in the out-of-control behavior of all humankind (1:18–32).

In these verses, then, Paul vents his own hot frustration with those fellow Jews whose behavior constitutes a threat to the Gentile mission. He does so in language current among Christians and shaped by the Old Testament. He also sees this very resistance as itself indicative of God's wrath; that is, he interprets the resistance as a sign of God's impending judgment.

In no sense does this passage imply that Paul has himself ceased to be a Jew. Later he will describe himself as "a member of the people of Israel, of the tribe of Benjamin, a Hebrew born of Hebrews" (Phil. 3:5), and in Romans also he insists on his own standing as an Israelite (11:1; see also 9:1–5). Quite apart from the explicit claims, Paul's constant recourse to the language and presuppositions of the Old Testament reveal that he does not stop being a Jew because of his belief that Jesus is Messiah. Even in this letter, in which there is little overt use of the Old Testament, his indebtedness to Jewish tradition is nevertheless apparent, as in this very passage.

Preaching a Difficult Text

Whatever we make of 2:14–16 in its context, it is necessary for the contemporary church to ask what to do with this and other passages in the shadow of the Holocaust and all that it reveals about the extent of Christian anti-Judaism. It may be instructive to notice what Paul does *not* say. He does not claim for the church the right to judge and condemn Jews or anyone else. The wrath that he refers to is God's own, not that of any human being. Nor does he claim that Jews have no right to exist. In other words, even those who would wish to read this passage literally and apart from its connection with Romans 9—11 need to respect the limits of the passage. Even taken at their worst, these lines in no way permit the outrages Christians have committed against Jews.

Many preachers and teachers will look the other way, hoping this text will pass. The Revised Common Lectionary diplomatically omits the troublesome verses, listing 2:9–13 as the epistle lesson for Proper 26, Year A. Congregants do read, however, and may well wonder what to make of verses 14–16. Given the deeply ingrained and too often unrecognized nature of Christian anti-Judaism, church leaders have the responsibility to address this question regularly. To say nothing about

38

these troublesome verses abdicates responsibility for them to those who will readily speak hate-filled words.

However this passage is used or avoided in preaching and teaching, it sounds themes of developing importance in the letter. One of those is the urgency of Christian proclamation. When Paul identifies the "hindering" of the apostles with displeasing God and even with killing Jesus and the prophets, he reveals the importance of the apostolic task. What is at stake here is nothing less than the rescue of humankind (1:10). In Paul's view, then, those who would interfere with Christian proclamation are displeasing to God.

These verses also reflect an assumption that human beings are responsible to God for their behavior. However verse 16 is translated, that conviction clearly underlies it. This assumption becomes more dominant in chapters 4 and 5, but it is introduced here.

The eschatological framework heightens the urgency of Christian proclamation and the responsibility of persons before God. Whatever the connotation of "at last" in verse 16, the reference to God's wrath is a reference to the impending eschaton, which Paul introduces in 1:10 and about which he will have much more to say later in the letter. The imminence of Christ's return renders proclamation of the gospel not only necessary but urgent. Christ's return also heightens the need for responsible behavior among those who wait.

Separation and Reassurance

1 THESSALONIANS 2:17—3:13

Having reviewed the initial stage of the Christian mission in Thessalonica, Paul now turns to more recent events. First, he recalls how he and his coworkers were separated from the Thessalonians, a separation that caused much anguish and finally led Paul and Silvanus to send Timothy to visit (2:17—3:5). Paul expresses his present relief and gratitude when Timothy returns with a good report (3:6–10). The prayer of verses 11–13 marks the end of this section of the letter and prepares the way for the ethical instruction in 4:1–12.

The Acts of the Apostles presents a more elaborate account of these events. Luke does not mention Timothy during the mission in

Thessalonica, although presumably he is understood to be included (see Acts 16:1–5; 17:14). Luke reports that Paul and Silas (Silvanus) fled Thessalonica because of the uproar there over Christian preaching, and they went immediately to Beroea (Acts 17:10). After Thessalonian Jews follow the group to Beroea and bring their outrage along, Paul is taken to Athens for safety. Silas and Timothy remain behind in Beroea. They reappear only when they rejoin Paul in Corinth (18:5).

Reconciling Paul's letter with this version of events in Acts is exceedingly difficult (see Introduction). Luke says nothing of a trip to Thessalonica by Timothy alone. Nor does Luke describe a time during which Silvanus and Paul were together in Athens without Timothy. Either Luke is simply misinformed about these matters, or both Paul and Luke omit the very details we need in order to reconcile events. Whatever took place, what is at stake here is far more than a travelogue.

1 Thessalonians 2:17—3:5
We Could Bear It
No Longer

Even the most cursory reading of this passage makes it clear that Paul does not write simply to remind the Thessalonians of what has happened since his departure. Perhaps the most outstanding feature of this text is the way it interweaves a straightforward account of events with highly emotional interpretative remarks and asides. "We wanted to come to you" yields to "certainly I, Paul, wanted to again and again. . . . " And "When I could bear it no longer" precedes "I sent to find out about your faith."

The "facts" acquired from reading 2:17—3:5 are minimal: the apostles were separated from the Thessalonians, that separation finally caused such anguish that they sent Timothy to visit. Not only does little information emerge here, but such information as appears must have been well known already to the Thessalonians. In common with the crafters of love letters, Paul does not write to convey data but to express his affection and communicate his concerns. Here three issues dominate: the connection between the apostles and the Thessalonians, the role of Satan, and the inevitability of persecution. All of these factors come together in verse 5, where Paul makes it explicit that he has been deeply concerned about whether the Thessalonians would be able to persist in their faith.

Apostles as Orphans (v. 17)

The passage opens with another of those astonishing metaphors for the apostles; Paul says that he and his colleagues were "made orphans." The NRSV supplies "by being separated from you," words that do not appear in the Greek text. Although the addition does not conflict with the passage, it explains away the metaphor and thereby reduces its impact. Scholars often comment that what Paul means is simply that the apostles were separated from the Thessalonians or even that they were made child*less* by the separation, again diminishing the force of Paul's colorful language. He and his colleagues became *orphans*. It is instructive that Chrysostom, who stands far closer to Paul's Greek than do modern commentators, insists on just this interpretation:

> He has not said "separated" but what was much more. . . . Because he had said above, "as a father his children," "as a nurse," here he uses another expression, "being made orphans," which is said of children who have lost their fathers. . . . For if any one should examine our longing, even as little children without a protector, having sustained an untimely bereavement, long for their parents, not only from the feelings of nature itself, but also on account of their deserted state, so truly do we too feel.
>
> ("Homilies on Thessalonians," 334)

One reason for this intense sense of connection between the apostles and the congregation becomes explicit in verses 19–20: "For what is our hope or joy or crown of boasting before our Lord Jesus at his coming? Is it not you?" As he will do in later letters also, Paul takes the faith of the churches he has founded and nourished as evidence of his own apostleship (see 1 Cor. 9:1–2). Even more, the churches fund his own profound joy and even pride (see also Phil. 2:16; 4:1; 2 Cor. 1:14; 7:4, 14; 8:24; 9:3).

The eschatological element here cannot be overlooked. Although it would be quite mistaken to say that Paul's own salvation at the Parousia *depends* on the standing of his churches, he nevertheless anticipates presenting these churches to the risen Lord as evidence of his faithfulness (see also 2 Cor. 1:14). Here the letter's ongoing concern with the Parousia focuses on the apostles themselves.

In one sense, this statement reveals anxiety on Paul's part. Had the Thessalonians in fact succumbed to "the tempter," Paul would experience a personal loss of significant proportions. In another and more profound sense, however, Paul signals a rather astonishing degree of confidence. In many of its stories and strands, the Bible assumes that the presence of God is an awesome, frightening event. The terrifying

41

epiphany at the Parousia is no exception to that generalization. For Paul to claim that he anticipates standing "before our Lord Jesus at his coming" with glory and joy reflects great assurance not only about the character of his work but about his vindication before God.

Satan's Interference (v. 18)

The Parousia is not yet a present reality, of course, nor is God's victory complete, for God's enemies are still at work in the world. The apostles could not return to Thessalonica because "Satan blocked our way," and Paul feared that the "tempter" might have successfully lured the Thessalonians. Later letters refer to Satan with similar suspicions. Satan is an enemy who attempts to outwit the faithful (2 Cor. 2:11; cf. 1 Cor. 7:5) and Paul's own "thorn in the flesh" was sent by Satan (2 Cor. 12:7).

Speculation about exactly what prevented Paul's return and how Paul came to identify it with Satan is just that—speculation. It is similarly pointless to wonder how it is that Satan could interfere with Paul's travel plans but not with those of Timothy. Luke's account would lead us to think that Thessalonian Jews pursued the apostles to Beroea, but numerous problems arise in reconciling the two accounts (see above). In any case, claiming that Satan prevented his return is a retrospective interpretation of whatever took place. Just as the church looks back and understands that certain events could only have taken place under God's care, so it understands other events to have been the work of God's enemy.

Perhaps it is as important here to notice what Paul does not say as what he does say. He does not offer a sociological interpretation for his inability to return to Thessalonica (i.e., "The Roman Empire is too strong for me!"). Nor does he interpret things psychologically (i.e., "Our enemies were jealous of our great gains in Thessalonica"). For Paul, this is an apocalyptic battle involving implacable enemies, and they will fight over every inch of terrain. That is to say, Paul interprets this situation theologically.

Just as Satan interfered with the return of Paul and his colleagues, Paul fears that the Thessalonians may have been tempted (v. 5), presumably in the face of persecution (v. 3). Paul's great fear for the Thessalonians is that they would "be shaken." In Paul's letters, the word persecution (Gr. *thlipsis*) often has the connotation of eschatological tribulation, suffering endured by the faithful at the hands of others (e.g., Rom. 5:3; 8:39; Phil. 1:17). The wording of verse 5 ("I was afraid that somehow the tempter had tempted you") suggests that these persecutions may be temptations to defection rather than physical attacks as such. It may be that new believers found themselves besieged by families and associates who were hostile to their faith. They may have found themselves pressed to continue in religious or social practices that were incompatible with the comprehensive claims of the gospel. They should have been prepared for such eventualities, because they know they are inevitable ("this is what we are destined for") and because Paul had warned them in advance.

The emotional language that runs through this passage is so powerful as to discomfort readers, even readers at the distance of twenty centuries. Many will attempt to deal with the affect here by dismissing it as rhetorical flourish or sheer manipulation (and there may be little doubt that Paul was trying to maneuver the Thessalonians). Others may respond by sentimentalizing the passage into a sweet reflection on Christian love. Neither response does justice to a text that reveals Paul's concern for a group of believers who are endangered by the presence of evil in the world.

Although this passage does not appear in the Common Lectionary, it affords preachers and teachers an excellent opportunity to reflect on how we talk or avoid talking about evil in the world. An understandable squeamishness steams up the conversation when people refer to Satan, since such talk can be a way of denying responsibility and self-discipline (as in Flip Wilson's all-purpose excuse, "The devil made me do it!"). And, just as Christians disagree about God's intervention, they also disagree about Satan's. We pay a high price, however, for our unwillingness to speak about evil, for by so doing we implicitly deny that it exists (see "Reflection: The Persistence of Evil," pp. 118–20 below).

1 Thessalonians 3:6–10
Timothy's Return

English translations cannot do justice to the rush with which Paul pours out verses 6–7. In Greek, these two verses constitute one long and very awkward sentence, in which all of verse 6 comprises subordinate clauses that lead up to the main verb ("we have been encouraged") in verse 7. A rough paraphrase might be, "With Timothy's return and with his report about you and your concern for us (just as we are concerned for you), we have been much encouraged. . . ."

The circumstances of Timothy's return are lost to us, although scholars sometimes attempt to wring from "just now" a precise reckoning of

43

the time elapsed. What is instructive is the way in which Paul "overwrites" verse 6. Given the context in verses 1–5, he need not say that Timothy has come "from you," and it is certainly redundant to specify that he came both "to us" and "from you." Earl Richard suggests that these phrases identify a new role for Timothy; he was sent to the Thessalonians as the representative of Paul and Silvanus, but he returns as the representative of the Thessalonians (*First and Second Thessalonians*, 157–58).

Paul first characterizes Timothy's report as "the good news of your faith and love." The verses that follow explain precisely what Paul means by "your faith and love," taking the two in reverse order. The second half of verse 6 concerns love, specifically the love of the Thessalonians for the apostles. That love is manifest in their constant recollections and their desire to see the apostles.

Beginning with verse 7, Paul takes up the faith of the Thessalonians and its impact. Paul does not elaborate on what exactly he means by "faith." The Greek word *pistis* can refer to faith in the sense of belief (as, for example, in 1 Thess. 1:8; Rom. 4:5) or to faithfulness (as in Rom. 3:3; Gal. 5:22). Here the context suggests an emphasis on the latter, especially in view of the language about standing firm in verse 8. Of course, it would be a mistake to distinguish sharply between the two senses. What the Thessalonians are faithful to is precisely the Christian faith they acquired from the apostles.

Paul's use of personal pronouns underscores the importance of the Thessalonians' faith. At the end of verse 7, he reports on the encouragement of the apostles "through your faith." Although English translations necessarily obscure it, the word order here is distinctive. Elsewhere in the letter Paul speaks of, literally, "the faith of you," (1:8; see also 3:2, 5, 6, 10). Here the order itself suggests emphasis: "through *your* faith." In addition, in verse 8 he supplies an emphatic pronoun in the phrase, "if *you* continue to stand firm in the Lord."

The faith of the Thessalonians does not benefit only themselves, however. One prominent feature of Paul's remarks is that the Thessalonians' faith serves to encourage the apostles in the midst of their own difficulties. Just as Paul has earlier reported that the belief of the Thessalonians has become "an example for all believers in Macedonia and in Achaia," so here their faith has buoyed the apostles themselves. The faith of the Thessalonians is not only their private belief, or even their corporate belief, something that matters only within their circle. It also belongs to the apostles and the rest of the church as well; the health of one congregation's faith matters for others.

44

The result of that faith for the apostles comes to exuberant expression in verse 8 with the report that "we now live, if you continue to stand firm in the Lord." Hyperbole enters in Paul's letters, not only in polemic (as at the end of chapter 2) but also in expressions of affection. Here he voices his relief at Timothy's news, and he sounds like the concerned parent with whom he compared himself in 2:1–12. Now that the crisis has passed, he breathes again.

This reflection on Timothy's report concludes with yet another affirmation of thanksgiving (v. 9) and with the prayer that Paul may see the Thessalonians again (v. 10). So much do these verses repeat earlier comments that we might skip right over them, except for the odd note at the end of verse 10: Paul prays that he and his colleagues may "restore whatever is lacking in your faith." Up to this point in the letter Paul has said nothing to suggest that there are deficiencies in the faith of the Thessalonians, so this comment raises a question about what exactly Paul has in mind.

We may find a hint regarding that question in 3:6. Notice that Paul says Timothy has brought news of the Thessalonians' "faith and love." What he does not mention is hope, although the opening thanksgiving identifies hope, particularly hope "in our Lord Jesus Christ" as a characteristic of this community. In itself this omission means little, but the fact that he goes on to speak about their kindly remembrance and their faith raises the question: What has become of their hope?

In view of the discussion in 4:13–18 of Thessalonian believers who have died, Paul may have in mind here their confident hope (or the lack thereof) in the Parousia. Some crisis in Thessalonica has caused severe questions about what the future will bring and who will be in that future, and Paul fears that this is a threat to their faith. This fear may explain why the theme of Parousia plays frequently in this brief letter.

1 Thessalonians 3:11–13
A Concluding Prayer for Love

These verses mark the transition from the first half of the letter, with its reflection on the apostles' mission at Thessalonica and its aftermath (1:1—3:13), to the second, which more directly concerns ethical matters (4:1—5:28). Paul has already reported in verse 10 on his ongoing prayer to be restored to believers in Thessalonica, but he utters a formal "prayer-wish," a prayer couched in the optative mood (the language of the strong wish) rather than in the imperative mood. Such

45

prayers appear elsewhere in the Pauline epistles, often at climactic moments in the argument (1 Thess. 5:23; Rom. 15:5–6, 13, 33; see also 2 Thess. 3:5, 16).

This particular prayer-wish consists of three petitions. First, Paul reiterates the prayer that God and the Lord Jesus might direct him to the Thessalonians (v. 11). Second, he prays that the Lord will increase the Thessalonians' love for one another and all (v. 12). Third, he prays that they may be strengthened (v. 13).

Several features of this prayer attract readers' attention. Verse 11 is unusual because nowhere else does a prayer-wish deal specifically with the desire of Paul to visit a group of believers. This desire has figured so prominently in the letter that it should not be surprising to find it here, however.

The manner in which Paul refers to God and Jesus in verse 11 is also striking, both because of the precise way he refers to God ("our God and Father himself") and because the Greek verb translated "direct" is singular rather than the expected plural. Paul more often describes God as the father of Jesus (Rom. 15:6; 2 Cor. 1:3; 11:31). The presence of the singular verb might be taken to mean that God and Jesus are so closely identified as to be one agent, but such a conclusion better fits the later language of the christological creeds than it does this early letter of Paul.

Perhaps an explanation lies in the way Paul speaks about God and Jesus in the remainder of the prayer. First, Paul refers to God and then to the Lord Jesus. Then, in verse 12, he addresses his prayer to the Lord. Finally he returns to standing before God at Jesus' coming. In other words, the two are not identified with one another here, but their activities are closely associated.

It is, of course, not surprising that Paul refers once again to the return of Jesus ("at the coming of our Lord Jesus with all his saints," v. 13). What is striking is the petition that the Thessalonians might be preserved in holiness and blamelessness. Paul has already said that he and the others were blameless in their conduct among the Thessalonians (2:10). And his claim that Jesus rescues "from the wrath that is coming" surely contains more than a hint that the Parousia brings with it accountability for behavior (see 1:10). Still, that concern has not emerged explicitly until 3:13, signaling the move to the discussion of blameless behavior in 4:1–12.

Although he does not say so directly, one implication of this series of prayers in verses 11–13 is that Paul knows that Satan's power is not uncontested! This section of the letter (2:17—3:13) opens with an assertion about Satan blocking the way (2:18) and the danger of the

46

tempter (3:5), but it closes with invocations of God to open the way again and to strengthen the Thessalonians. Whatever power Satan possesses is real, but Paul believes that it will prove no match for the power of God. It is God alone who will finally triumph.

It should not surprise anyone to find this transitional passage couched in the language of prayer. By so doing Paul reveals once again his profoundly theological convictions. Paul and his colleagues will not return to Thessalonica simply by planning their itineraries more carefully. Nor will the Thessalonians experience enhanced community life or moral practices because they will themselves to do so. These things come about not as achievements but as gifts of God.

Although this section of the letter commends itself for the preacher, the Revised Common Lectionary includes only verses 9–13 (for First Advent in Year A), and, without the preceding context, that section consisting largely of prayers will be difficult for people to grasp. Hearers of the text may feel a bit as if they are visitors in a strange church, trying to understand various petitions in the pastoral prayer. It may help either to read the preceding section (beginning with v. 17) or at least to provide clues that give Paul's prayer specificity.

What prompts the selection of this text for Advent, of course, is the brief reference at the conclusion of the prayer to the Parousia of Jesus, for tradition understands that Parousia as the Second Advent. And, read on the First Sunday of Advent, the motif of eager expectation comes to the foreground of this passage. The eagerness with which gathered believers anticipate once again the Advent of Jesus mirrors the eagerness with which Paul and his colleagues longed to be reunited with the Thessalonians.

Preachers who develop sermons on this passage elsewhere in the year may confront a temptation to turn it into a tirade against ministers who do not love their congregations enough or congregations who do not love their ministers enough. Such a reading fails to see the way in which this text emphasizes the vulnerability of the Christian preacher and teacher. The connection forged with those who are congregants or students is such that church leaders are themselves highly susceptible if those in their "charge," so to speak, turn aside.

Put somewhat differently, this passage pushes all believers to acknowledge the corporate character of Christian faith. Faith is not something that belongs to the individual or even the local congregation or church. Faith is public in that the beliefs and actions of individuals influence others. Paul may be speaking hyperbolically when he says "we now live, if you continue to stand firm," but he reveals something

47

central to Christian faith and life. This is not an arena in which the rejoinder, "What I believe is my own business!" can be recognized and respected.

For the teacher, this might prove an excellent opportunity for raising the question of the horizontal (relations in community) versus the vertical (relations to God) dimensions of faith. So often that question arises as people contemplate the Bible in ways that pit one dimension over against another, as, for example, when James's demand for good works competes with Paul's theme of justification by faith. Here that strategy falls by the wayside as Paul completely integrates these two aspects of faith. Because of God's actions, the apostles and the Thessalonians are irretrievably connected with one another. And that connection causes them to give praise to God. Neither dimension exists apart from the other.

Concerning Lives That Please God

1 THESSALONIANS 4:1–12

It is conventional to refer to this passage as opening the "ethical" section of the letter (4:1—5:24), as I have done in the introduction to this commentary. That designation is convenient and, to a certain extent, appropriate, for here Paul addresses questions of behavior in a direct manner. The distinction can also be misleading, however. Chapters 1—3 of 1 Thessalonians are profoundly ethical in that they recount events in ways that implicitly urge the Thessalonians to continue as examples for others (1:6), maintaining their steadfastness in faith (3:1–5) and their love of one another (3:6, 12). In addition, this "ethical" section is also profoundly theological, because Paul's instructions stem from his convictions about who God is and what God is doing and will do in the world (4:7, 14; 5:9). To make a sharp distinction between the two is to misrepresent Paul's thinking about the gospel itself, for Paul sees theology and ethics as inextricably intertwined.

48 Following an introductory appeal for behavior that is pleasing to God (vv. 1–2), the passage consists of instructions on sexual immorality (vv. 3–8) and general admonitions about life in community (vv. 9–12).

Although the subject matter of verses 3–8 appears strikingly different from that of verses 9–12, the unit as a whole is connected both formally and in its underlying concern. Formally, the unit begins and ends with reference to the way in which the Thessalonians are supposed to "walk," translated "live" in verse 1 and "behave" in verse 12. The presence of the same Greek verb (*peripatein*) at the beginning and ending of the passage ties the passage together in a literary *inclusio*.

In addition, as the discussion of the passage will show, one concern that connects these two sets of instructions is the relationship between believers and unbelievers. Paul warns against sexual conduct like that of "the Gentiles who do not know God" (v. 5) and encourages proper conduct "toward outsiders" (v. 12). What emerges here is a need to encourage behavior that will strengthen the small and struggling community of believers in Thessalonica, setting around it boundaries that will protect it and yet make it attractive to others who might be called to share Christian convictions.

1 Thessalonians 4:1–2
Instructions through the Lord Jesus

These introductory verses overflow with appeals designed not only to get the attention of the readers or hearers of the letter but also to persuade them to take seriously the discussion that follows. "We ask" becomes "we ask and urge." Twice Paul makes reference to previous instruction in these matters ("as you learned from us," and "you know what instructions we gave"). Appeals are made both to the name of the Lord Jesus and to pleasing God. The Thessalonians are commended for following these instructions but are also urged to increase their efforts. Nothing in the discussion that follows in 4:1–12 suggests that the Thessalonians have failed in a significant way, for Paul is not elsewhere hesitant to point out such problems and rather directly (as in 1 Cor. 5:1–8). He evidences, nevertheless, the same sort of anxiety that characterizes his treatment of the Thessalonians' faith in chapter 3. They live in a world hostile to Christian convictions, a world that will make Christian life a precarious undertaking.

Paul's reference to previous instruction offers a rare glimpse of the content of early Christian preaching and teaching. What he and his

49

colleagues took to Thessalonica was not a story of salvation that began and ended in the heavens and never engaged questions of human behavior. Neither was ethical instruction an afterthought. Theology and ethics were thoroughly intertwined even at the beginning.

The subject of the apostles' instruction was "how you ought to live and to please God." The two infinitives work together to convey a single demand (technically known as a verbal hendiadys), namely, that Christians live in a way that pleases God. Earlier in the letter Paul reminds the Thessalonians that he and his colleagues conducted themselves "not to please mortals, but to please God who tests our hearts" (2:4; see also Gal. 1:10). Paul does not counsel indifference to what others may think or feel (as is clear in Rom. 14:1—15:13 and particularly in the discussion of food offered to idols in 1 Corinthians 8—10), but his primary concern is with behavior that pleases God rather than with pandering to the unreliable standards of the day.

What exactly Paul means by urging "in the Lord Jesus" (v. 1) and giving instruction "through the Lord Jesus" (v. 2) remains unspecified. It seems unlikely that he has in mind teachings that come directly from Jesus himself, since Paul's letters make little reference to the life and teachings of Jesus, speaking instead about the cross and the resurrection. Even when he comments on the imitation of Jesus (as in 1 Thess. 1:6), he refers to general patterns of behavior rather than to specific actions or beliefs. Almost certainly, then, "in the Lord Jesus" and "through the Lord Jesus" refer to the space Christians occupy, their location; that is, Paul makes his appeal as one who is "in the Lord Jesus" to those who are also "in the Lord Jesus."

This motif emerges prominently in later letters, of course. In Gal. 3:28, Paul designates believers as those who are "one in Christ Jesus," having been baptized with Christ and no longer constrained by the divisions that marked the old age. In 1 Corinthians 12:12–31, he expands on this phrase as a means of talking about the corporate character of faith. All believers constitute one body that is "in Christ." Although it would be too much to claim that the full resonance of this phrase already is heard in 1 Thessalonians 4:2, this passage may well anticipate later developments.

An additional feature worth noticing in these verses is that they offer no promise of a reward in exchange for an acceptable moral life. No carrot swings from the end of this text. Paul assumes that believers want to please God, not that they do so in order to get the prize at the bottom of the box. In Paul's view, behavior flows forth naturally in gratitude to the God these Gentiles have turned to serve (1:9).

1 Thessalonians 4:3–8
The Call to Holiness

Paul signals the importance of what he is about to say by identify-ing it in solemn language as "the will of God, your sanctification." The terseness of Paul's language here frustrates attempts to understand precisely the relationship between "the will of God" and "your sanctifi-cation." The interpretation is complicated by the way in which Chris-tians often confuse sanctification with striving for moral perfection. In Greek, sanctification (*hagiasmos*) is simply a noun related to the adjec-tive "holy" (Gr. *hagios*) so that it may also be translated "holiness" or consecration. Paul refers to believers as "saints" or "holy ones," not be-cause they are extraordinarily good but because God has made them holy (see, for example, Rom. 1:7; 1 Cor. 1:2; 2 Cor. 1:1; Phil. 1:1). What is particularly striking in this passage is that holiness—sanctification, consecration—is associated not with going out of the world or observ-ing special rituals but with the basic human business of sexual conduct.

Control of
Which "Vessel"? (v. 4)

With the warning against fornication and its explanation in verse 4 we encounter a complicated problem of translation. According to the NRSV Paul urges the Thessalonians to control their own bodies, but those familiar with the RSV will recall that it reads "that each one of you [should] know how to take a wife for himself in holiness and honor." The startling difference between the two translations stems from a debate about how best to render a particular Greek noun and the verb used with it. The noun that divides the two translations is *skeuos*, which literally means "vessel," as in the mundane "jar" of Luke 8:16 or 2 Corinthians 4:7. Clearly the word carries a figurative connotation here, but there is some question as to what exactly it "figures." Complicating matters is the fact that the verb used with *skeuos* is *ktaomai*, which normally means to acquire something (as in "take no gold . . . " in Matt. 10:9; see also Acts 8:20) but sometimes means to possess something. The question, then, is whether Paul refers to using ("possessing") the vessel of one's own body (as in the NRSV) or to acquiring the vessel of a wife (RSV).

This debate did not arise in the second half of the twentieth cen-tury with questions of inclusive language. At least as early as the fourth-century church fathers Theodore of Mopsuestia and Augustine, we find disagreements about how to understand Paul's wording here.

51

Advocates of the position that Paul means "wife" appeal to 1 Corinthians 7:2, where Paul says that "because of cases of sexual immorality, each man should have his own wife and each woman her own husband." They also cite the use of *skeuos* in 1 Peter 3:7, where the wife is the "weaker vessel" (NRSV: "weaker sex"). In addition, they point to language about men taking wives in Tobit 4:12–13, Ruth 4:10, and Sirach 36:29 (see also Prov. 5:15–18 and Sirach 26:12) and to some later rabbinic texts in which women are described as "vessels."

The view that *skeuos* means "wife" also can appeal to the well-established notion in the ancient world that the sexual behavior of a woman is a commodity in the possession of her husband or, if she is unmarried, of her father or brother. Given that assumption, engaging in sexual intercourse outside marriage involves violating the property rights of another male. On this reading, verse 6 refers to the injustice done a male when another male engages in sexual intercourse with a woman whose sexual activity "belongs" to him. (The "and sister" of v. 6 is, as the note in the NRSV indicates, an addition the translators make because it is assumed that Paul's customary address of believers as "brothers" includes both women and men in the church.)

Advocates of the other major position, that Paul means "self" here, note that in 2 Corinthians 4:7 the term *skeuos* (NRSV: jars) refers to the fragile human person and that 1 Peter 3:7 says that the wife is the *weaker* vessel, not that only the wife is a vessel. They also note that the rabbinic texts in which women are referred to as "vessels" come into written form only several centuries later than Paul and that the Old Testament texts cited do not use the term vessel. In addition, 1 Corinthians 7:2 not only refers to a man having a wife but also to a woman having a husband, reflecting a mutuality missing from this text if the translation "wife" is preferred.

Those who argue that Paul means "self" here can also appeal to the conviction that is found in any number of Greco-Roman texts (including Jewish texts) that sexuality is something that must be controlled. Some medical writers insist that sexual intercourse actually harms the body. The first-century Cynic Musonius Rufus associates sexual excess with "the life of luxury and self-indulgence":

> Men who are not wantons or immoral are bound to consider sexual intercourse justified only when it occurs in marriage and is indulged in for the purpose of begetting children, since that is lawful, but unjust and unlawful when it is mere pleasure-seeking, even in marriage. But of all sexual relations those involving adultery are most unlawful, and no more tolerable are those of men with men, because it is a monstrous thing and contrary to nature. But, furthermore, leaving out of

consideration adultery, all intercourse with women which is without lawful character is shameful and is practiced from lack of self-restraint.

(Fragment 12)

In other words, Paul may have been issuing only the most conventional sort of plea for self-control. (Such comments reveal little about how Jews and Gentiles actually conducted themselves, of course. Pronouncements on sexuality are notoriously unreliable indicators of human behavior; they tell us what the pronouncers value but not whether anyone listens or conforms.)

This brief sketch of a complex debate is sufficient to show that real difficulties accompany either approach. It may be wisest to leave the passage ambiguous by translating *skeuos* simply as vessel. Whatever Paul means in this particular text, it is certain both that Paul was opposed to adultery and that Paul was opposed to all sexual expression outside of monogamous marriage (see 1 Cor. 6:15–20; 7:1–2).

It is important to see, however, that one reason this debate has emerged is precisely that *Paul himself gives us few clues* as to what he means by the use of the word *skeuos*. He writes in terse aphorisms that call out for explanation. Presumably this is because he has already instructed the Thessalonians, and they know what he means, even if we do not (see vv. 1–2).

The Nature
of Holiness (v. 7)

If we let go of the need to solve the translation problem and momentarily read "around" the disputed phrases, an interesting thing happens. What comes to the foreground is the language of "holiness and honor," the warning about engaging in lustful passion like that of "the Gentiles who do not know God," the warning about God's role as judge. What becomes urgent here is not the question of *who* rightfully engages in sexual relations but *how* those relations are to be conducted. They are to be characterized by "holiness and honor."

A bit of polemic makes the admonition sharper. Believers are not to be like *those* Gentiles, the ones who are unbelievers. Here Paul draws on an element of traditional Jewish polemic about sexual promiscuity among the Gentiles, as he does also in Romans 1:18–23. The author of the Wisdom of Solomon engages in this same polemic:

> Then it was not enough for them to err about the knowledge of God,
> but . . .
> they no longer keep either their lives or their marriages pure,

53

but they either treacherously kill one another, or grieve one another by
   adultery,
and all is a raging riot of blood and murder, theft and deceit, corruption,
   faithlessness, tumult, perjury,
confusion over what is good, forgetfulness of favors,
defiling of souls, sexual perversion,
disorder in marriages, adultery, and debauchery.

(Wisd. Sol. 14:22–26)

An absurd form of this same prejudice appears in some later rabbinic discussions about the conversion of Gentiles, in which certain rabbis assume that a female proselyte over the age of three years and one day (*sic*) must already have been used sexually. In other words, "everyone knows" what Gentiles do. (Such passages tell us nothing about sexual behavior among Gentiles, of course, but they do reveal the fears of some Jews.)

Ironically, as noted earlier, some Greco-Roman writers would have agreed about the dangers of unbridled sexual conduct and advocated monogamous sexual relations. That in itself raises a perplexing question. If other moral teachers of the day—including *Gentile* moral teachers—offered these same instructions regarding sexual conduct, how can Paul urge the Thessalonians to comply with his instructions so that they will *not* be like those Gentiles?

This anomaly points to an important dynamic in the passage. By insisting that Gentile converts conduct themselves sexually "in holiness and honor," and "not like the Gentiles," Paul is drawing an invisible boundary around the community. He is marking it off from the rest of the world, so that it will survive the very threats he has already referred to in chapter 3.

In this sense, Paul's strategy is a bit reminiscent of the mother who stands at the door and calls out as her child scampers off to play, "Behave yourself! Remember you are a Smith!" Without ever being explicitly told what it means to *be* a Smith, the child learns that her behavior is to be consistent with that identity. Down the street, other children with different names *hear the same admonition*. They may even hear an additional warning, "We are *not* like those Blakes! Don't act like them! Behave!"

In addition, even if Paul's admonitions resemble those of his contemporaries, his reasoning differs sharply. When Musonius Rufus insists on the importance of sexual self-control, he does so in order to preserve the dignity and honor of the individual. Musonius is concerned about the consequences for the life of the person engaged in sexual misconduct. By contrast, Paul's language about accountability to God is sharp: "the Lord is an avenger in all these things," "God did not call us to impurity but in holiness." The Christian acts, not out of concern for his or her honor, but for the pleasing of God.

Particularly important is Paul's concluding comment in this section (v. 8): these instructions come from God who gives the Holy Spirit. The NRSV interprets this contrast between the human and God as one of authority, although the Greek text does not include a word for authority. Paul may have in mind something other than human versus divine authority, however; the "human" may refer either to Paul and his colleagues (in the sense of their teaching authority) *or* to those brothers and sisters who stand to be wronged by sexual immorality. In either case, what is at stake is more than what human beings think or the rights of any human being to another's sexual conduct. Although it is important not to do harm to others, as verse 6 makes clear, what is at stake is nothing less than the will of God (see v. 3).

The identification of God as the one "who also gives his Holy Spirit" seems an odd digression. Although this is Paul's first reference to the Holy Spirit since 1:5–6, it is important to recall the language of verse 3 regarding "sanctification" or "holiness." Holiness is not a goal to be achieved by dint of the human will or initiative, but because God *gives* that spirit of holiness. Perhaps this reference to the Holy Spirit also anticipates 5:19 ("Do not quench the Spirit"), as well as reminding the Thessalonians that it is the Spirit that enables them to live "in holiness and honor" with one another.

Discussion of this passage will prove a diplomatic challenge in many Sunday school classes. Given the combination of tradition, cultural assumptions, and personal experience that shapes Paul's admonitions *and* the various combinations of tradition, cultural assumptions, and personal experience present in any random group of Christian adults, the reaction may be explosive. A teacher might well begin by simply pointing out the ways in which our vantage points differ from those of Paul. (For example, most North American Christians do not, at least not consciously, consider women's sexual conduct within the legal category of property rights. Nor are unbelievers assumed to be wildly promiscuous.)

It may be helpful also to pay careful attention to the theological assumptions Paul brings to this discussion. Perhaps one difficulty with the discussion about sexual morality in our churches is that we decry certain behaviors (or we quietly overlook some that were once regarded as abhorrent, such as premarital sexual intercourse), but we do so without attention to the underlying theological issues. We operate out of a psychological model, discussing whether premarital sexual experience is

55

healthy or unhealthy for marriages. Or we deal with questions from a strictly social perspective, expressing concern about the impact on youngsters who grow up with only one parent and the fact that the parent is too often young and inexperienced. These are certainly appropriate concerns, but they are not sufficient because they do not touch the question: What is it that is pleasing to God?

Teachers and preachers might also explore the question: What does it mean to engage in sexual intercourse "in holiness and honor"? Recent discussion of sexuality in North American churches has sometimes focused so exclusively on the identity of the partners that nothing has been said about the quality of the sexual relationship itself. Surely there are married sexual relationships that are abusive, in which the treatment partners render each other has little to do with holiness and honor.

1 Thessalonians 4:9–12
Philadelphia
(The Love of Brothers and Sisters)

At first reading, this passage resembles an airplane that cannot make it off the runway. Paul spends a great deal of energy to "rev up." He introduces the topic of love among believers at the beginning of verse 9, but only in verse 11 does it acquire any specificity. First he explains that the Thessalonians do not need written instructions, then that they have been taught by God directly, and then that they in fact do love all believers throughout Macedonia. But, just in case, he adds, "do so more and more."

Such a long introduction has a rhetorical effect of underscoring the importance of what follows. When Paul says that "you do not need to have anyone write to you," he is employing a rhetorical device known as paralipsis, in which a speaker draws attention to what he is about to say by claiming that he will not dwell on it. We might find the equivalent in such comments as "I won't say a thing about how late you were last night," or "This year we won't even talk about money during the Stewardship Campaign."

Oddly enough, when Paul does turn to specific instructions in verse 11, he sounds like a precursor of Ann Landers or Abigail Van Buren: "Live quietly, mind your own affairs, work with your own hands." These

lines could be torn from the pages of a modern handbook for success-
ful living rather than quoted from the Bible. Or we might find them offered for sale at a local craft show, needlepointed onto a delicate little
pillow that has been decorated with flowers.

Before giving up on this passage as hopelessly mundane, we need
to attend a bit more closely to the language used and the way the admonitions are related to one another and to the context. The general
topic of Christian love is so familiar to us that we scarcely notice it when
introduced in verse 9. Paul has already recalled the love of the Thessalonians (1:3) and warmly identified Timothy's report as "news of your
faith and love" (3:6). Here, however, he speaks specifically about a topic
known as "love of the brothers and sisters" (Gr. *philadelphia*). Most
uses of this term in texts prior to Paul concern the love of biological siblings for one another, but in New Testament writings it rather quickly
comes to be applied to the relationship among believers (Heb. 13:1;
1 Peter 1:22; 2 Peter 1:7). Given the extensive use of familial terminol-
ogy in this letter (e.g., 1:4; 2:7, 11; 4:1, 13), it should not surprise us that
Paul characterizes the affection of believers for one another as that of
siblings.

Paul does say two things about this sibling love that are surprising.
First, the Thessalonians have been "taught by God" to love one another
(v. 9). The Greek word translated "taught by God" is *theodidaktoi,* and
it may be a word of Paul's own creation, since it appears nowhere else
until after Paul's letters. Isaiah 54:13 does look forward to the day when
"all your children shall be taught by the Lord," but the wording of the
Septuagint differs from Paul. The claim that the Thessalonians are
"taught by God" is a curious one, raising the question of how it is that
people can be said to have God directly as their teacher. The reflection
on the Thessalonians' experience in chapters 1—3 suggests that God has
taught them love in that God has loved them ("beloved by God," 1:4),
not unlike the Johannine insistence that Christians know how to love one
another because God has loved them (e.g., 1 John 4:7–21). In addition,
the apostles, themselves sent by God, have modeled *philadelphia*
(2:1–12), and the gift of the Spirit instructs the Thessalonians (1:5; 4:8).

Paul's insistence on this point is noteworthy, for "you yourselves"
is emphatic in the Greek as in the NRSV. That the Thessalonians have
been taught by God does not negate earlier comments about the apostles as teachers of the Thessalonians (2:12; 4:1–2), but it emphasizes the
Thessalonians' own rightful place within the community of faith. It also
puts them at odds with those contemporary prophets of self-sufficiency
such as Epicurus, who claimed to have been self-taught. Paul knows
better. The claim to be self-taught is sheer hubris.

57

The second surprising comment regarding love within the community appears in verse 10 with Paul's enthusiastic observation that the Thessalonians "love all the brothers and sisters throughout Macedonia." Even allowing for Paul's customary hyperbole, this claim seems preposterous. What does it mean to speak of a group of believers in one city loving all those in the entire region? Indeed, it means little or nothing, if by "love" we mean what we usually mean by "love": a sentimental attachment or personal affection. Given the evidence from Paul's letters about the conduct of his labor, however, he may understand love in terms of intercessory prayer, financial support, and hospitality. All of these actions of love were essential for early Christian mission, and all stem from a profound sense that believers in one place are connected to believers elsewhere. Such love does not exclude the love of those outside the community (see 3:12). Even if Paul's eye at the moment falls on the conduct of Christians with one another, one reason for strengthening relationships within the community is to maintain the goodwill of those outside (v. 12; compare 1 Cor. 14:16, 23).

With verse 11 Paul turns from general exhortation about love to specific directions about conduct: "aspire to live quietly," "mind your own affairs," "work with your hands." All have parallels in the philosophical writers of the day. The first two admonitions are associated with withdrawal from political involvement and public life. One who lives "quietly" does not seek public attention or political power; similarly, philosophers often contrasted minding one's own affairs with being a busybody.

Paul's concern about work is anticipated earlier in the letter. As early as the thanksgiving, Paul recalls the Thessalonians' "work of faith and labor of love." In 2:9, as he remembers the visit of the apostles, he claims that they worked "night and day," and in 3:3 he reports on his own worry that his labor in Thessalonica might have been in vain.

This admonition also has parallels among the philosophical teachers, but the attitude toward skilled or manual labor is complex. Cicero dismisses as vulgar "the means of livelihood of all hired workmen whom we pay for mere manual labor, not for artistic skill" (*On Duties* 1.150–51). Others, however, such as Plutarch and Dio Chrysostom, advocate manual labor for those in need. Not surprisingly, the attitude toward work varied according to social location. Some of those in Paul's churches who were of relatively higher social standing may have disdained his practice of self-support through labor (see 2 Cor. 11:7–11), while others found the same practice affirming of their own lot in life.

58

Verse 12 provides the motivation for these admonitions: "so that you may behave properly toward outsiders and be dependent on no one." It is unclear whether Paul is concerned not to offend those on the outside of the community or whether he hopes to attract them. The particular instructions of verse 12 appear to have as their goal the sort of restrained lifestyle that would not prompt criticism by outsiders. The willingness to work would render believers able to supply their own needs.

As already noted, such admonitions may be found frequently among the writings of the popular philosophers of Paul's day. As in verses 3–8, however, Paul's admonitions differ in their motivation. Paul's instructions have to do with pleasing God (v. 1), constructing a community life consistent with the gospel. That feature of the text becomes clear when we see the movement between verses 9–10a and verses 10b–12. Paul's general language about love of brothers and sisters becomes concrete in the specific instructions in verses 10b–12. Love of one's fellow believers involves behavior that is responsible and seemly, both in order to avoid criticism from outsiders and in order not to strain relations within the community.

As in verses 3–8, another major concern here in verses 9–12 is with the boundary around the community of believers. The language of family earlier in the letter is intensified here with the term *philadelphia.* The boundary extends to include all those believers throughout the region of Macedonia. The reference to "outsiders" respects the judgments of those outsiders, but it also marks the line between outsiders and insiders.

The pressing question that remains is why Paul raises (indeed, repeats, for he says he has already told them these things) these issues here. The fact that similar concerns appear again in 5:13–14 suggests that these are not simply general concerns that he would introduce everywhere; they may reflect some specific tendency in Thessalonica. Is there a tendency among the Thessalonians to think that Christian life exempts one from the concerns of proper sexual conduct, from responsible labor, from right behavior to others within and without the community? Some may have interpreted the news that Jesus Christ rescues believers (1:10) as license to do whatever they liked.

Such license to irresponsibility might intensify among a population convinced that Jesus would return at any moment. Scholars have often argued that the admonitions in 4:11 are necessary because the Thessalonians (or some of them, at least) believed they no longer needed to work or conform to community standards of any sort. Paul does not, in this passage, refer to the Parousia, but its dominance as a theme in this letter makes such a possibility reasonable.

59

Confronting Paul's
Ethic of Holiness

The Revised Common Lectionary omits this passage, and reasons for that decision are not hard to surmise. Few preachers will relish the opportunity to talk about fornication during the Family Hour on Sunday morning, and those who do will do so badly. And the injunctions to "live quietly" and "mind your own affairs" can easily be reduced to a lack of concern about others, which is anything but what Paul has in mind. Simply discarding this text will not address the problem, however.

Whether or not the preacher decides to address this passage in a sermon, it is a provocative passage in several respects. First, the passage reveals something important about Paul's approach to ethical considerations. Paul does not urge ethical behavior in order to produce a morally perfect individual or an honorable, virtuous life. Paul is not writing a self-help manual on the achieving of a happy, productive Christian life. The moral life is sought not for the sake of the individual's good or even for its own sake but for that of serving and pleasing God.

Second, this concern about ethical behavior is integrally related to the task of creating and sustaining community. What distinguishes Paul from Dio Chrysostom and many others is that the quiet life is not the private life. Paul's concern that Christian behavior should set the community apart from the world around it challenges our comfortable absorption of church into the category of "voluntary organization." And, to be sure, Christians have sometimes taken their "set apartness" to extremes that become abusive. Yet it is important to contemplate whether anything can be said about boundaries around our communities of faith. Does it matter in any way whether people worship and pray and participate in Sunday school? What makes those people, individually and corporately, different from their peers?

Third, Paul assumes that our bodies—our persons—belong to the God of creation. What provokes contemporary readers in this and similar passages is the underlying claim that we are not free to do as we please with our bodies. If Paul does not here say, "You are not your own," as he does in 1 Corinthians 5:19, that assumption is nevertheless at work. Behavior, sexual or otherwise, is a matter for which all human beings, as created by God, are accountable to God. This assumption will surely encounter resistance in many corners of North America, where the ethic of the autonomous self reigns unquestioned. As uncomfortable as it may be to do so, this passage offers preachers and teachers an excellent occasion for pressing the question of why Paul might say such things. His understanding of creation stands behind them; that is, if we believe that God created us, then we remain obligated to do what pleases God. We do not belong to ourselves, and no amount of protest will make it so.

Fourth, the passage may stimulate thinking about strategies for preaching and teaching on ethical issues. Paul's strategy here is quite straightforward (that is not always the case in his letters, as in Romans 14 when he refuses to take sides between the "weak" and the "strong," urging each group to respect the other). He offers rules and makes clear appeals to his own authority. Many of us would find ourselves uncomfortable with such approaches to authority; we would also find them counterproductive in a society that has grown highly intolerant of authority and authority figures. Often people who hear preachers or teachers say, "You must do so and so," or "You must *not* do so and so," will simply turn the proverbial deaf ear. Others, of course, crave rules precisely because they appear to make things tidy, a bit like coloring within the lines.

None of these complicating factors permit teachers and preachers to abdicate their responsibility. Perhaps the place to start is with the persistent exploration of Paul's most basic assumption: we are creatures of God and not at liberty to do as we please.

Comforted and Challenged by the Return of the Lord

1 THESSALONIANS 4:13—5:11

From the opening lines, the Parousia of Jesus Christ permeates this letter. Believers are those who "hope in our Lord Jesus Christ" (1:3) and who "wait for [God's] Son from heaven" (1:10). God calls believers into God's "own kingdom and glory" (2:12); Paul prays for their blamelessness at "the coming of our Lord Jesus with all his saints" (3:13). If this concern is muted briefly during 4:1–12 (although note the reference to the Lord as avenger in 4:6), it now reemerges in explicit and prominent fashion. There is no escaping the importance of eschatological language in this letter. To read 1 Thessalonians without taking seriously the conviction of the Parousia and its importance is to read with blinders fastened securely in place.

61

This major section of the letter comprises two closely connected passages. In the first (4:13–18), Paul takes up a serious pastoral problem created by the deaths of believers in the Thessalonian community. The second (5:1–11) specifically concerns the character of the expectancy that is to mark the Christian response to the impending eschaton. The two passages are connected not only by the subject matter of the eschaton but also by their pastoral concern. Each concludes with the assurance that believers will be with their Lord (4:17; 5:10), and each closes with the admonition that believers should encourage one another (4:18; 5:11). These words of assurance and exhortation stand at the heart of the letter's message.

This passage poses special problems for interpretation. Although contemporary Christians may cozy up to the friendly language that dominates chapters 1—3 and perhaps welcome (or at least tolerate) the ethical instructions in 4:1–12, here we enter what seems to be a land of terror and foreboding. The heavens are above; they contain Jesus who will descend; strange and loud sounds will announce him, and believers will be caught up in the air to Jesus. To many modern readers, this is not the language of consolation but of fairy tale, and interpreting it requires careful attention both to the language itself and to its rhetorical function.

1 Thessalonians 4:13–18
Comforted by the Hope
of the Lord's Return

With its introduction of "those who have died," verse 13 clearly marks a change in topic. Despite persistent reference to the Parousia, this is the letter's first discussion of the implications of that event for those believers who have died. "We do not want you to be uninformed" does not necessarily imply that Paul regards the Thessalonians as completely ignorant on the topic. As with the expression "our coming to you was not in vain" (2:1), he may be employing litotes, so that the statement can be paraphrased, "We want to be sure that you completely understand this matter."

Paul's succinct introduction of the topic, "those who have died," raises many questions about precisely what has caused grief among the Thessalonians. A variety of explanations have been offered, ranging from a gnostic-like denial of the resurrection, to the abrupt interruption of Paul's teaching, to anxiety that those who have already died might be disadvantaged by being absent at the Parousia. The simplest explanation, given the early date of this letter and the evidence in the text, is that the community did not expect anyone to die prior to Jesus' return. Paul's earliest instruction in Thessalonica included Jesus' resurrection (as 1:9–10 surely indicates) and possibly even the resurrection of the dead. For the Thessalonians, the Parousia seemed so imminent that they believed none within the community would die before Jesus' return. The deaths of believers have now occurred, however, prompting a trauma. What can it mean that believers have died, and what will happen to those believers at the Parousia? The answer Paul provides is both theological and pastoral.

Paul begins by distinguishing the Thessalonians once again from those who surround them, "so that you may not grieve as others do who have no hope." The language is ambiguous. It can refer either to those who have no hope for their own futures (that is, they will not themselves be resurrected to salvation) or to those who do not hope in the future return of Jesus. The second nuance is preferable in this context, even if Paul will shortly refer to those who are children "of the night" (v. 5) and raise the possibility of being "destined for wrath" (v. 9). At present, however, Paul is so concerned with offering assurance to believers that he has little to say about others beyond the boundary of the community. More important, earlier in the letter "hope" refers to the hope believers have in the Parousia of Jesus (1:3 and 2:19), and that is the preferable interpretation here also.

Jesus' Triumphant Return (v. 14)

Paul makes a crucial shift in verse 14. Having introduced the problem of death and grieving for the dead, he might have been expected to write a letter of consolation, such as those written by his contemporaries. Those letters address the problem of grief through appeals to reason and dignity. For example, Plutarch writes to a friend whose son has died, urging reason as the best cure for grief, in recognition of the fact that all people are mortal (*Letter to Apollonius* 103F–104A). Seneca similarly appeals to reason, but he also scolds a friend for his unseemly display of excessive grief ("You are like a woman in the way you take your son's death," *Epistle* 99.2). By striking contrast with Plutarch and Seneca, however, Paul appeals to the promise of Jesus' triumphant return as Lord of all. In that event Paul finds consolation, not in self-discipline and restraint.

63

Verse 14a ("Jesus died and rose again") may well be a creedal formula. Several features of the statement prompt this conclusion. First, the introductory words, "we believe that," assume that the statement that follows is already well-known to the Thessalonians. Second, the sheer economy of words ("Jesus died and rose again") is consistent with the notion of traditional language that has been pared to the essentials. Third, the formula speaks of "Jesus" rather than Paul's more customary "Jesus Christ" or "Christ Jesus." Finally, the formula affirms that Jesus "rose" (Gr. *anistēmi*) rather than that Jesus "was raised" (Gr. *egeirō*), which is Paul's preference elsewhere (see, for example, Rom. 4:24–25; 8:11; 1 Cor. 15:4; 2 Cor. 1:9). Paul inherits this formula, perhaps one with which the Thessalonians were already familiar, and employs it here as the basis for an affirmation about Christian hope.

The connection between the two parts of verse 14 is clear, although implicit. Those who believe that Jesus died and rose again also believe that Jesus will return: "even so, through Jesus, God will bring with him those who have died." The language of verse 14b is torturous. What Paul says, translated literally, is, "thus also God those who slept through Jesus will bring with him." Both of the prepositional phrases torment translators. "Through Jesus" may refer, as the NRSV takes it, to the manner of God's action; that is, God will act through the agency of Jesus. On the other hand, "through Jesus" may refer to the ones who have died in the sense that they died in Jesus (see, as a parallel, those "who have died in Christ," 1 Cor. 15:8). Since the passage otherwise makes it quite clear that Jesus is God's agent (v. 16), it seems likely that "through Jesus" refers to the identification of those who have died rather than to Jesus as God's agent.

"God will bring with him" is also extremely awkward. Does this statement mean that God sends Jesus who brings along those who have died (but see v. 16), or does it mean that God brings together (in the sense of causing to come together) Jesus and those who have died? The picture is by no means clear. Perhaps the difficulty arises because Paul wants to affirm both God's priority *and* Jesus' central role. He manages to do so, but the result is grammatically challenging.

However frustrating this statement is for translators, its theological relationship to verse 14a is clear: Jesus' resurrection is not an isolated event, a single rabbit God pulls out of the hat to demonstrate that Jesus is in fact the Christ. The resurrection is directly connected with God's final triumph and with the lives of all human beings. This is consistent with Paul's treatment of the resurrection elsewhere. As Ernst Käsemann put it:

64

Paul only spoke of the resurrection of Christ in connection with, and as the beginning of, the resurrection of the dead in general. . . . As the overcoming of death it is for [Paul] the beginning of the rule of the one with whom the kingdom of divine freedom begins.

("The Saving Significance of the Death of Jesus," 55)

A Matter of Precedence? (v. 15)

With verse 15 Paul takes up a specific feature of the resurrection of the dead. Those who remain alive at the Parousia will not have precedence over those who have died. There is no advantage for those who remain and no disadvantage for those who have died. By contrast with what he will later write in Philippians 2:23 and 2 Corinthians 5:1–9, here Paul does not say that the dead are already with Christ Jesus.

Paul introduces this teaching with solemn language: "this we declare to you by the word of the Lord." Some scholars have understood the "word of the Lord" to refer to a specific saying of Jesus, but nothing in the Gospels closely parallels the statements that follow (although frequently Matt. 24:29–44 is invoked). Probably Paul does not have in mind a specific saying of Jesus but is speaking with confident authority born of his apostolic call (see 2 Kings 13; Sirach 48:3). In that sense, the statement says no more than what Paul has already said in 1:5 and 2:2–4; this community believes itself to be instructed, in an ongoing fashion, by the will of the risen Lord.

It is important to notice that Paul says, "We who are alive, who are left until the coming of the Lord." Apparently he was convinced that the Parousia would come so quickly that some believers would remain alive until Jesus' return (see also 1 Cor. 15:51 and compare Mark 9:1). It is this same sense of the impending nearness of the Parousia, of course, that helps us understand why the Thessalonians may have responded with utter dismay to the death of believers in their midst.

Lord of Heaven and Earth (vv. 16–17)

Verses 16 and 17 concretize the assurance of verses 14–15 with a brief and explicit scene depicting the return of the Lord. The language is replete with conventional apocalyptic imagery (although Paul's scenario is tame when compared with the fantastic imagery of *1 Enoch* or even Revelation). The descent of the triumphant Lord recalls Daniel 7:13 as well as the use of the Daniel text in Mark 14:62.

65

A loud shout, a mighty trumpet, or other great sounds from heaven characterize apocalyptic passages (for example, 2 Esdras 6:23; Dan. 10:6; Rev. 1:10; 14:2; 19:6). Similarly, angels and archangels figure prominently in apocalyptic texts (for example, 2 Esdras 4:36; *1 Enoch* 20:1–8), as do references to the clouds of heaven (*1 Enoch* 14:8; Dan. 7:13).

Although this language may have been colloquial for Paul's contemporaries, it is a wholly foreign tongue to most of us. We may find ourselves trying to parse out the relationship between the cry and the call and the trumpet. Does the sound wake the dead or only precede them? Exactly what happens to those who are caught up into the air? Where do they go next?

Questions such as these threaten to reduce Paul's language to production directions for the halftime show at the Super Bowl. They also miss the point. This passage has more in common with poetry than with blueprints. That does not mean we do not take it seriously—or that Paul does not mean it seriously. But the importance of this account lies in its underlying logic rather than in the specifics. The seriousness of apocalyptic language lies less in the details than in the dazzlement of the vision as a whole.

The logic at work here has to do with power and who has it. The Gentile Thessalonians may not have been familiar with all the apocalyptic motifs at play in the background of this text, but they did know about power and could not have missed its vocabulary. Here Paul paints a scene involving nothing less than the arrival of the Lord of heaven and earth.

The trumpet does not merely begin the overture to a pretty drama being acted out on stage; it announces the arrival of a royal figure, and may also sound a call to battle. Similarly, the notion of "meeting the Lord in the air" speaks the language of power. The word "meeting" (Gr. *apantēsis*) is used of a ruler paying an official visit or the return of a conquering hero of war (see also Matt. 25:6). This particular dignitary receives tribute, not outside the city gate, but "in the air." That Jesus is "in the air" signals that his dominion is not that of an earthly ruler. Unlike the Roman emperor, he is not in charge of particular territories. He is in charge of all territories.

By virtue of this powerful entry, the "dead in Christ" will rise up. Then those who remain alive will be "caught up" to meet the Lord. The verb translated "caught up" is quite graphic and might well be translated as "snatched." Paul employs the same verb in 2 Corinthians 12:2 and 4. More important, perhaps, other writers speak of death as "snatching" its victim away from life. Here, it is not the enemy death snatching away living victims but Christ snatching away from death those who belong to God.

The scene culminates in the astonishing claim: "and so we will be with the Lord forever." In this context of the crisis at Thessalonica, Paul offers profound consolation. To be "with the Lord" is to be safe, as is clear in the parallel statement in 5:9–10 (compare Rom. 8:31–39). To be with the Lord is to be beyond the reach of evil, remote from the touch of pain. This is also a further claim about the Lord's power, since only power could make such a promise.

We do not find here the battle imagery of Revelation or even the language about defeating God's enemies in 1 Corinthians 15. Paul's main concern is not with the defeat of rival powers; nevertheless, the text makes some not entirely subtle claims about who has real power.

Consolation Empowered

On the basis of this evocative scene and promise, Paul writes simply, "Therefore encourage one another with these words" (v. 18). Paul does not discourage grief with pious nonsense to the effect that Christians should not grieve because they know their loved ones will be with God. Instead he recognizes the reality of grief, but distinguishes the Christian's grief from that of others who do not know the hope of the Lord's return. One mark of the Christian community, then, is its particular understanding of grief and its peculiar comfort.

Preachers and teachers will find much to address in this passage. The question of how we deal with eschatological texts is of obvious significance (see "Reflection: Preaching and Teaching Eschatology," pp. 76–79 below). Numerous other issues come to the surface here, however.

One concern common to every congregation is the need for consoling those who grieve. As already noted, a characteristic of Greco-Roman literature at the time of Paul and letters of consolation is their obsession with moderation in grief. Someone who grieves overmuch is unseemly, out of control, so the writer will attempt to attenuate the grief by persuasion that death is inevitable and should be accepted. Strategies have not changed dramatically despite the passage of two millennia. People observe that the deceased has gone to a better place, or take solace from the fact that she no longer suffers, or speak about him looking down on us from heaven. In other words, people in desperate pain will seek and grasp for comfort wherever they can find it, in an effort to manage the pain of loss. Paul takes a strikingly different strategy. He places the story of those who have died within the context

67

of what God is doing in the world. Their story has meaning as part of God's story.

That Paul uses theology for comfort food might seem, at first glance, odd. An examination of most any order of worship for a funeral service will confirm, however, that the strategy has proved lasting. If the church does not often use this particular passage from 1 Thessalonians, it does read 1 Corinthians 15 and Romans 8, passages that also look to the future triumph of God. Perhaps that is because we too know that death is the implacable enemy, and it is comforting to remember that death is not only our enemy but God's. The promise that God has already begun to triumph, that finally God will prevail, makes the otherwise unbearable somehow bearable.

Some will object that the comfort Paul offers here is merely "pie in the sky by and by." In one sense, that's the only kind of comfort there can be, the assurance that someday things will not hurt the way they do now. However, Paul does not instruct the Thessalonians to be moderate in their grief or to cease manifestations of grief. Instead, he urges them to reframe it, to see its relationship to the future God intends.

Another issue might be the ministry of believers in community with one another. To "encourage one another" is not to assign to one leader the task of caring for the pastoral needs of all church members. And it is certainly not to leave individuals and families isolated in their grief. The exhortation to "encourage one another" (see also 5:11) places the responsibility for a ministry of consolation squarely within the community.

The Revised Common Lectionary assigns this passage near All Saints' Day (Year A, Proper 27), which is particularly appropriate. What Paul affirms regarding the relationship of believers with one another and with their Lord reaches well beyond a social relationship confined to this time and place. Those who are bound together in this community remain so, even after death. The boundary Paul has drawn around the church is a boundary that extends into the future. Although a boundary separates believers from nonbelievers, it does not separate the living from the dead. The social world created in the church runs in two directions—believers' association with their Lord and their association with one another.

Interpreters also may reflect on what it means for the church to proclaim the future triumph of God without being triumphalistic. Most basically, it means always remembering that the triumph belongs to God and not to humankind. It is neither in the possession of the church nor, as the next passage makes emphatic, is it under the church's control.

1 Thessalonians 5:1–11
Challenged by the Hope
of the Lord's Return

Initially, Paul's shift from 4:13–18 to 5:1–11 jars us. So abrupt is the movement that scholars sometimes suggest that 5:1–11 must be an interpolation. The two passages very much belong together, however. The Parousia that Paul promises in 4:13–18 may be trusted, but it cannot be predicted. It comes quickly, with no one's knowledge, and under no one's control. In other words, having confidence in Jesus' return is one thing, but naming the day is another. Consistent with other New Testament writers, Paul insists that no one knows when that day will be (see, for example, Mark 13:32; Acts 1:7).

As is often the case in Paul's letters, tracing the movement of this passage is crucial for understanding what he has to say. Paul begins with a reminder about the "time and the seasons," that is, the hiddenness and suddenness of the Parousia (vv. 1–3). Then he insists that the crisis of the day of the Lord does not threaten believers, for they are "children of the day" (vv. 4–5). Then he considers what it means to be "children of the day" and to live accordingly (vv. 6–8). He concludes with a reminder about the destination God plans for these children and with words of exhortation (vv. 9–11).

The passage begins with the now familiar direct address to the "brothers and sisters," and with the rhetorical claim that the Thessalonians need no instruction on the matter of "times and seasons." As in 4:9, Paul employs paralipsis, drawing attention to his new subject matter by claiming that he will not speak about it. The topic itself, "times and seasons," is a shorthand expression for the timing of the eschatological events (as in Dan. 2:21; 7:12; see also Acts 1:7; 3:20–21). Not surprisingly, a common feature of apocalyptic writings is the question, "When will these things happen?" (see, for example, Dan. 12:6; 2 Esdras 4:33; 6:7; *2 Baruch* 24:4; 26:1).

The Day of the Lord

Perhaps the Thessalonians have themselves pressed Paul (either in writing or through Timothy) for specifics or engaged in speculation about the timing of the Parousia. He scarcely even acknowledges the question of timing. "You yourselves know very well" what the answer is: "the day of the Lord will come like a thief in the night." Presumably, the Thessalonians already know what Paul means by "the day of the

69

Lord," although they may not know that in the Old Testament it refers to the anticipated day of judgment (as in Isa. 2:12–22; Jer. 46:10; Ezek. 30:2–3; Amos 5:18–20; Zeph. 1:14–18) and that early Christians applied the reference to the Lord to Jesus Christ.

What Paul has to say about this "day of the Lord" in verses 2–3 is terrifying. He says little about when it comes but everything about how: it comes "like a thief in the night." Other New Testament texts compare the arrival of the Parousia with a thief (2 Peter 3:10; Rev. 3:3; 16:15), but only Paul adds "in the night" (although see Matt. 24:43 and the parallel in Luke 12:39). The addition serves to increase the power of the comparison: Who is not afraid of the thief? And specifying that the thief comes *at night* multiplies the anxiety, for night is the realm of that which needs to be hidden, which is out of control, utterly unpredictable.

Verse 3 explains why this image of the thief at night is so disturbing. It is exactly when people believe they have achieved "peace and security" that devastation follows. The challenge of this language extends well beyond the individual householder, who may believe that the house is well-protected and the goods are safe. Rome proclaimed itself as the advocate of peace and declared security through its own agency. The enthusiastic first-century historian Velleius Paterculus articulates the viewpoint:

> On that day [the rise of Rome] there sprang up once more in parents the assurance of safety for their children, in husbands for the sanctity of marriage, in owners for the safety of their property, and in all men the assurance of safety, order, peace and tranquillity.
>
> (*Compendium of Roman History* II, 103.5)

Despite all precautions, the day of the Lord comes, and with it comes sudden destruction (Jer. 48:3–6; Hos. 9:6; Ezek. 6:14; 15:16). It comes as inevitably as the pangs of labor come upon a pregnant woman (see Isa. 13:8; *1 Enoch* 62:4; 2 Esdras 4:40–43). Relentlessly Paul piles up these images, familiar from prophetic and apocalyptic works, as he moves toward the verdict: there is no escape! Just as a woman cannot escape the labor involved in giving birth, neither can anyone escape the day of the Lord.

Darkness and Light

70   Suddenly, in verse 4, the language shifts again. Paul abruptly changes from the third person depiction of the day of the Lord to the direct address to the "beloved." The fear invoked by verses 2–3 has no

power over the Thessalonians, for they "are not in darkness" and cannot be surprised. Describing the day of the Lord is left aside in favor of describing the people of the Lord as "children of light and children of the day," not "of the night or of darkness." The terror of verses 2–3 has no power over them.

The contrast between believers and those on the outside, harsh as it sounds to modern ears, would have been familiar to many of Paul's contemporaries. The Jews at Qumran spoke of themselves as the children of light and castigated those "born of falsehood" who come from the darkness (1QS 3:13–15, 20–21; 4:18–19, 22–23). Other early Christian writers share this notion of Christians as the children of light (see Luke 16:8; John 12:35–36; Eph. 5:8). For Paul in this context, the darkness of night as the realm in which a thief operates has become the realm of darkness that stands over against God's realm and God's rule.

By employing this imagery, Paul once again marks an implicit boundary around the community. The point is not to castigate, or even to identify, those who belong to the night, but to re-present to the Thessalonians their rightful concern and their rightful identity. Paul is too consumed with the task of nurturing this fragile community of faith to be caught up with condemning those on the outside. And, as becomes quickly apparent in verses 6–8, the language of light and darkness serves both to identify believers with one another and to encourage appropriate behavior.

The imagery of light and darkness occurs in a vast array of ancient texts, and the reasons for that are readily apparent. The darkness conjured up is that of night in a world that could not imagine instant, reliable illumination of the night. The contrast between day and night, light and darkness, was as dramatic a contrast as Paul could imagine. In no sense does he refer to skin color when he speaks of darkness, and it is to the church's great shame that such associations have been made. Precisely because our world assumes the presence of light even in the midst of night, however, preachers and teachers need to make clear the arena in which Paul's language works.

Verses 6–8 use the contrast for exhortation. Since believers belong to the day, they should remain awake, sober, watchful. The exhortation culminates in verse 8 with the introduction of a different sort of imagery, that of armor (the breastplate of faith and love, the helmet of the hope of salvation). This change of language connects the passage with the triumphant imagery of Christ's return in 4:13–18. Believers may be the "children of light," those who know that Jesus will ultimately return in triumph, but that does not mean that the present is anything less than a struggle.

71

Unfortunately, the NRSV seriously misleads readers with its translation of this verse, a translation that makes the taking on of armor into an admonition ("Let us be sober, and put on . . .). By contrast, the Greek indicates that believers already wear these items, so we might better translate, "Since we are children of the day, clothed with the breastplate of faith and love, and as a helmet the hope of salvation, let us be sober." The distinction is by no means trivial; the NRSV suggests that believers select these items for themselves, as if they willed themselves to be the recipients of the gospel and its armor. This insistence on the armor as something received rather than chosen seems confirmed by the fact that, in the Old Testament passages where similar imagery occurs, it is the Lord who dons the armor. For example, "He [the LORD] put on righteousness like a breastplate, and a helmet of salvation on his head" (Isa. 59:17; see also Wisd. Sol. 5:18; compare *T. Levi* 8:2; Eph. 6:14–17; 2 Cor. 6:7). If the armor belongs to God, then the only way it can be worn by humans is that God has granted it to them.

The triad of faith, love, and hope recalls the thanksgiving of the letter (1:3; and compare 3:6, where hope seems deliberately omitted). At this point in the letter it has become clear that faith, love, and hope are not randomly chosen Christian virtues, and, still less, mere emotions. Faith is confidence in the gospel itself, the confidence that leads these Gentiles to turn to serving God (1:9–10). Love embodies that faith in concrete actions both within the Christian community and beyond it. Hope, as we have seen throughout the letter, is the firm expectation of the return of Jesus Christ.

Living with the Hope of Salvation

The reference to "the hope of salvation" also provides an important transition to verses 9–11, the very heart of the passage. Here Paul reminds the Thessalonians that God has planned for their salvation, and he appeals, on the basis of that plan, for the Thessalonians to act accordingly. God's plan is "not for wrath but for obtaining salvation." The language replays important elements in the creed of 1:9–10, which anticipates God's wrath and Jesus as the divine agent who rescues humanity from that wrath. God's salvation of humanity comes about "through our Lord Jesus Christ, who died for us."

Paul says tantalizingly little here about the death of Jesus, but he says the essential, simply that it is on our behalf, "for us." Familiarity with the language of substitutionary atonement will incline many to read that doctrine into Paul's brief assertion, but it is by no means clear

72

that "for us" means that Jesus died in the place of sinful humankind. Paul does speak in those terms in passages in later letters, but he also speaks of the cross as "on behalf of" humankind in the sense that it reveals the way in which God acts in the world or the way in which God assesses the world.

Verse 10 returns once more to the vocabulary of waking and sleeping, but it does so in a confusing manner. Just a few verses earlier, Paul has drawn a sharp line between those who are awake (believers who are alert for the eschaton) and those who are asleep (unbelievers who have no idea what time it is). Here he reintroduces that vocabulary, but asserts that it makes no difference whether we are awake or asleep. To be sure, in the discussion of believers who have died, Paul employs the euphemism of sleep (see the note in the NRSV at 4:13), but the Greek word there is different. This raises the possibility that Paul means that both the morally alert and the morally asleep will "live with him." Despite the word choices in this verse, that is probably not what Paul wants the Thessalonians to understand, as he is in the midst of an extended exhortation to watchfulness and care in behavior. More important, the impulse of this verse is to remind the Thessalonians that salvation is in God's hands, not in human action.

The passage concludes with an expanded form of the exhortation of 4:11. These same words conclude a second-century letter of sympathy from an otherwise unknown Egyptian woman: "Therefore comfort one another" (Grenfell, ed., *The Oxyrhynchus Papyri* 1, no. 115). By contrast, the formal letters of consolation mentioned earlier in connection with 4:13–18 approach the problem of grief from something close to a "bootstraps" mentality. The bereaved individual is admonished to "behave" better—use reason, be sober, be restrained.

Paul expands on this admonition to encouragement with "build up each other." In the later Pauline letters, this motif of upbuilding emerges as an important criterion for decision making within the church. Worship is to be ordered for the upbuilding of the church (1 Cor. 14:5, 12, 17, 26), and judgments about individual practices are scrutinized by the question of what will make for upbuilding (Rom. 14:19). Here upbuilding is understood in more general terms and recalls the behavior of the apostles as described in 2:11–12, each believer being urged and encouraged to lead a worthy life.

Earl Richard observes that in a sequence of three passages Paul begins with misunderstandings or misplaced concerns of the Thessalonians and then reshapes those concerns in another direction (*First and Second Thessalonians*, 266). He begins with the Thessalonians' concern about love within the community and reframes it as a concern for all

73

(4:9–12). He reframes their grief for the dead as hope for the coming Parousia and life with the risen Lord (4:13–18). He reframes their concern for times and seasons as an admonition to watchfulness (5:1–11). Richard's identification of the Thessalonians' concerns may not be entirely persuasive, but he permits an important observation about the way in which Paul works as pastor and teacher, especially in 5:1–11. He begins with a particular issue of some anxiety, anxiety that he regards as unnecessary, perhaps even trivial. Rather than criticizing the Thessalonians for their anxiety, he lifts them beyond it, using the occasion for reframing their worry about the Parousia into moral energy and commitment to the larger community. The worry about "times and seasons" becomes first a word of assurance ("As the children of light, you need not worry"), then an admonition to act the part to which they belong, then a reminder: "Whether we are awake or asleep we may live with him." Instead of brushing off their concerns, he takes them seriously by interpreting them in a theological context.

These words have about them something of the comfort and assurance of Psalm 23. Whatever the circumstances, the shepherd will not abandon his flock but will find a way to care for them. Even death itself cannot remove God's people beyond the reach of God's care. This conviction reappears in Romans 14 in slightly different form with the words, "If we live, we live to the Lord, and if we die, we die to the Lord; so then, whether we live or whether we die, we are the Lord's." Here Paul makes a crucial move, both for this particular letter and for his thought as a whole: One cannot move beyond the care of God. In that light, fretting about time or the times becomes utterly wasteful.

The reassurance that so dominates this passage will not be entirely welcome, for it involves the recognition of God's sovereignty. It is God who has made decisions about the human future, and not human beings. This comes as an offense, not only or even primarily because we know the strange twists taken by some understandings of predestination. What Paul says is nothing more than that God is in charge. Yet it is precisely that claim that gives offense. Perhaps especially in the late twentieth century, the notion that God might be in charge, that God might have a plan, flies in the face of a world determined to set its own agenda.

In addition, the question that must be asked is who is the "us" in this text. When Paul writes, "God has destined *us*," is he leaving out the "them" over there? Certainly the dualism earlier in the passage suggests that there are those who inhabit the outside of the circle. Yet it would be a mistake to make this into a passage about us and them; it is, rather, a passage about what God has done, is doing, and will do for us. We have enough to do with worrying about how we live in response to that action without also worrying about whether our neighbors are on the inside or the outside. Those decisions belong to God, who is capable of making them; we are not.

What Time Is It?

In addition to the powerful reassurance of verses 9–10, preachers may find this text an intriguing place to reflect upon time. As so often in passages suffused with apocalyptic imagery, one of the questions at work here is who knows what time it is. Paul does not even bother to issue the reminder that the time is set by God alone (as is done in Acts 1:8, for example). Instead, he assumes that the Thessalonians know who owns the time. Any effort at predicting these times is, on the face of it, absurd.

Preachers may also find this passage a powerful witness to the notion of security—both true and false forms of security. Verses 2–3 touch on strategies of security that are both personal and corporate. To frustrate the "thief in the night," we rely on heavy-duty locks, flood lights, and alarm systems of increasing sophistication. We seek after "peace and security" in relationships, in wealth, in work, in national strength. Quite apart from an apocalyptic scenario, these are all strategies of self-delusion, for each and every one can be overturned in a moment. By contrast, the security Paul commends cannot be won or increased or even seen by human eyes. As the world measures "peace and security," the gospel has nothing to offer. Yet the reminder that "we will be with the Lord forever," that "awake or asleep we may live with him," means that the gospel is the only security anyone has.

For both preachers and teachers, this passage affords an excellent opportunity to reflect on the way in which we handle questions. If, as suggested above, Paul learned that the Thessalonians had concerns about the timing of Jesus' return, he might simply have answered their question directly. He might have said, "We do not know when the Parousia will take place. That's up to God, not to us. Next question?" That would have been a simple, direct, clear answer to the question. Paul's response, however, reflects an awareness that behind the request for information lurks another question, one that the Thessalonians may be unable to articulate. That lingering question concerns security. (What is the question about time, after all, but a question about security and how to achieve it at the right time?) Because he sees the question *behind* the question, Paul reframes the Thessalonians' concern in a way that allows him to go to the heart of the matter. Quite beyond the

75

subject under discussion in this passage, Paul's strategy encourages teachers and preachers to listen for the real questions, the ones people may be unable to bring to speech or even to consciousness.

REFLECTION:

Preaching and Teaching Eschatology

Perhaps few elements in the Bible present more difficulties for preachers and teachers than eschatological passages, those that anticipate the "last days." The graphic language of 1 Thessalonians 4:13–5:11, with its promise of "the archangel's call," "the sound of the trumpet," and "sudden destruction," may send otherwise intrepid exegetes scurrying for cover. Yet reading the New Testament without attention to these passages is a bit like selecting raisin toast for breakfast and then eating around the raisins. Eschatology may occupy the periphery of our understanding and experience, but it is not a peripheral matter.

One difficulty we face in this section of 1 Thessalonians, as in other eschatological passages in the Bible, is precisely the oddness of the language and imagery used. When Paul peers into the future and sees believers being caught up with Christ in the air, we scratch our heads and wonder how many clouds will be needed and how many believers each will support. When the author of the Apocalypse looks forward to "the new Jerusalem, coming down out of heaven from God" (Rev. 21:2), we contemplate ways in which Andrew Lloyd Webber might stage its descent. When Daniel asks, "How long shall it be until the end of these wonders?" (Dan. 12:6), we reach for long-range planning calendars.

That is not to assert that the "modern mind," with its scientific world view, has no tolerance for eschatological scenarios. Hollywood routinely offers up eschatological scenarios, whether instigated by nuclear holocaust (as in *The Day After*), by invaders from outer space (as in *Independence Day*), or by virulent disease (as in *Outbreak*). Perhaps the most elaborate of this genre is Stephen King's *The Stand,* in which a deadly virus wipes out most of the earth's population, following which the survivors serve as representatives of God in the final eschatological battle. If anything, the appetite for wild eschatological speculation in film and fiction makes the eschatological passages in the Bible seem tame, but it also makes them more puzzling. To put the matter directly: How is it that the Bible contains scenes so outrageous as to challenge the skills of the best special effects technicians?

Not all of the problems preachers and teachers face stem directly from the texts themselves. Christians who have preceded us and those among our contemporaries have offered interpretations of these texts that make many readers uncomfortable, if not forthrightly embarrassed. First Thessalonians 4:17 alone has sparked ferocious bickering over the "rapture" of the faithful: will it occur before the tribulations described in the Apocalypse, or only after them?

For preachers and teachers who want to explore eschatological texts with their churches, an excellent beginning point is reading other Jewish texts of Paul's era, in which eschatological speculation is routine. Leaving aside the New Testament texts, we might take up 4 Ezra (known in the NRSV as 2 Esdras 3–14), which is readily available in those editions of the Bible that include the Apocrypha (those works recognized as canonical by the Roman Catholic church but not by Protestants). Fourth Ezra, written late in the first century C.E., consists of a series of visions accompanied by interpretations. At one point the angel warns of a time when

> the sun shall suddenly begin to shine at night,
> and the moon during the day.
> Blood shall drip from wood,
> and the stone shall utter its voice;
> the peoples shall be troubled,
> and the stars shall fall.
>
> (4 Ezra [2 Esdras] 5:4–5)

Later the seer learns of the "day of judgment":

> a day that has no sun or moon or stars, or cloud or thunder or lightning, or wind or water or air, or darkness or evening or morning, or summer or spring or heat or winter or frost or cold, or hail or rain or dew, or noon or night, or dawn or shining or brightness or light, but only the splendor of the glory of the Most High, by which all shall see what has been destined. It will last as though for a week of years.
>
> (4 Ezra [2 Esdras] 7:39–43)

Other Jewish writings of this era reveal the diversity of eschatological concerns. *First Enoch* opens with a vision of the last day in which God marches upon Sinai, as a result of which the hills "melt like a honeycomb" and the land opens up and all the earth perishes. God's arrival is accompanied by "ten million of the holy ones" who will execute God's judgment (*1 Enoch* 1). The author of *2 Baruch* elaborates on the "twelve parts" of the coming tribulation, which include famine, earthquakes, ghosts, and rape, and culminate in "disorder and a mixture of all that has been before" (*2 Baruch* 27). Eschatology permeates the Dead Sea Scrolls, but the War Scroll is particularly striking with its

77

precise instructions for and descriptions of the final battle between the forces of light and those of darkness. *1 Enoch* and *2 Baruch* are available in *The Old Testament Pseudepigrapha*, edited by James H. Charlesworth, and the Dead Sea Scrolls in *The Dead Sea Scrolls in English*, translated and edited by Geza Vermes.)

Recognizing that Paul and other New Testament writers draw upon a common eschatological language helps to demystify these passages. Yet, like the adolescent's claim that "everyone else" is doing something, it does not answer the more fundamental question: What do these eschatological writings mean?

The answer to that question varies with different writings, of course. In 1 Thessalonians, as we have seen, Paul offers the eschatological scenario in chapter 4 to comfort the grieving and encourage the community in its faith. First Corinthians 15 appears to move in a different direction, where anticipation of the defeat of God's enemies underscores the imperative of faith in the power of God to secure that triumph begun in the resurrection.

Pastors who have read Romans 8 or 1 Corinthians 15 or Revelation 21 while looking upon faces etched in agony will readily understand this function of eschatology. In the funeral service, the church puts aside its sophistication and skepticism and shouts into the pit of death: "You will not have the last word. This life, and all life, belongs to God."

Eschatology does far more than comfort the grieving, although that may be when we understand it best. Eschatological language also gives voice to the conviction that not everything is the way it seems. In common with other early Christians, Paul rejects the notion that what we blithely refer to as "the real world" constitutes the final arbiter of the things that matter. He understands that this "real world"—namely, the views and virtues that dominate—does not have the final say. On Good Friday, when the "real world" appears to conquer, God already reveals that its decisions are utterly false. On Easter, God unmasks the pitiful weakness of this "real world."

This theological framework helps explain the bizarre character of much eschatological writing. The language must be bigger than life because it grasps after convictions that extend beyond life as it can be seen and touched and heard. Ordinary, clear, plain prose simply will not work.

That is not to relegate eschatology to the realm of ethereal speculation, however, with no consequences for the present. For Paul, eschatology has ethical implications, although not in the way people often assume. Paul does not urge believers to behave in a certain way so as to earn the carrot and avoid the stick. Instead, expectations about

78

Jesus' return make responsible behavior a matter of urgency. In 1 Thessalonians 5:1–11, for example, he does not exhort the Thessalonians to *become* "children of the day"; rather, he declares that they are and urges them to act accordingly. The fact of God's coming triumph enables believers to look frankly on the dirt and grime that surround them but to live expectantly, leaning toward the future.

Some will insist that "real" Christians must understand and accept the various eschatological scenarios found in the New Testament as if they were exact previews of coming attractions. A variety of factors— the elapse of two millennia, conflicts among various texts, a scientific mind-set, to mention a few—will make that affirmation exceedingly difficult for many people. On the other hand, the unshakable confidence that God is God and that the powers of the world will not have the last say is not marginal to the Christian faith. The language of eschatology is more theological and pastoral than predictive.

Conduct within the Community of Believers

1 THESSALONIANS 5:12–24

The final section of ethical instructions consists of an extended collection of specific exhortations (5:12–22), concluded by a prayer-wish (5:23–24), just as the prayer-wish of 3:11–13 brought the first major section of the letter (technically, the letter body) to a close. Because many of the specific exhortations are conventional, readers may find themselves rushing through this passage to finish the letter. Resisting that temptation is important since many of the letter's central themes (such as relationships within the community, the Parousia, the faithfulness of God) come together once again in these final lines.

At first glance, the admonitions in this section seem to possess all the coherence and logic of a grocery list. As the shopper walks out the door to the local market, another family member calls out, "And don't forget to buy carrots!" In similar fashion, Paul tacks on, "Abstain from every form of evil." Yet the grocery list may have its own sort of order, perhaps dictated by the arrangement of aisles in a familiar supermarket, and Paul's ethical instructions similarly have a kind of order. Verses 12–13 concern the proper attitude toward workers within the community, concluding with the very direct words, "Be at peace among yourselves." In verses 14–15 Paul turns to quite a different segment within the community, those who have grown discouraged or lax in their involvement. Verses 16–22 consist of terse commands, each of which has to do with community conduct, particularly conduct in worship. The admonitions culminate with a prayer-wish that both invokes God's protection and promises the community God's faithfulness.

Each of the subsections of admonitions combines some admonitions that appear to be entirely traditional (e.g., "See that none of you repays evil for evil," v. 15) with others that appear to address a particular situation at Thessalonica (e.g., "Do not quench the Spirit," v. 19). Any decision about which statement falls into which category is fraught with peril, of course, and interpreters need to acknowledge the problems inherent in such historical reconstruction. For the tasks of preaching and teaching, it is intriguing to see the freedom with which Paul employs traditional instruction to address a particular local situation.

Treatment of Leaders
(vv. 12–13)

Verses 12–13 exhort respect and esteem for "those who labor among you, and have charge of you in the Lord and admonish you." Given the emergence of the formal categories of clergy and laity in later decades of the church's life, readers may think immediately that Paul has in mind respect for the office of ministry. At this early stage, however, there are no official ministerial offices or authorizing procedures, and Paul's language includes all those who have leadership roles at Thessalonica. (One of the reasons Paul has to defend his apostleship elsewhere is that there is no official authorizing body, so that he must persuade others of the legitimacy of his calling as an apostle on a location by location basis and is subject to rejection on the same basis.)

Similar instructions appear in other New Testament writings (e.g., 1 Cor. 16:18; Heb. 13:17; and 1 Peter 5:5, where "elders" refers to leaders of the community), although none is as specific as this one. It is also striking that the language of work and labor appears again here, as it did in the thanksgiving (1:2–10) and in the recollection of the initial apostolic work (2:1–12). This repetition, together with the urging to peace at the end of verse 13, could mean that Paul has particular concerns about the Thessalonians and their treatment of leaders.

80 The additional remark, "Be at peace among yourselves," does not necessarily belong with the preceding remarks about respecting workers, although the rhetorical introduction to verse 14 ("And we urge you,

beloved") does set verses 12–13 apart from verse 14 and mark these two verses as a unit. Quite apart from this literary connection, the conjunction of respect for community laborers and the urging of peace is highly suggestive, raising the question of how a believing community can be at peace apart from a sense of respect and regard for its leaders. (See the similar imperatives regarding peace in Rom. 12:18; 14:19; and compare Heb. 12:14.)

Recalling that these verses have to do with all church leaders and workers and not only ordained clergy alone does little to prevent the train wreck when verses 12–13 collide with the contemporary mistrust of anything that smells even a little bit like authority. Having rightly rejected a naive trust in anyone associated with church leadership, many congregations have swung to the opposing extreme, treating leaders with a suspicion that borders on contempt. The saints of the congregation transmogrify into demons upon their election to the congregation's official board. Paul's words might well serve as the beginning point for sorely needed discussion about regard for ministers and lay leaders.

Treatment of the Marginal (vv. 14–15)

The transition at verse 14 is marked not only by the resumption of the initial direct address ("brothers and sisters" in v. 12 and "beloved" in v. 14 both translate the same Greek word, *adelphoi*) but also by a change of subject matter as Paul moves from the leaders in the community to those who inhabit its margins. He names three specific groups: the "idlers," the "faint hearted," and the "weak." Scholars sometimes try to identify these groups precisely, almost as if we could name the individuals who belong within each category. While avoiding such extremes in speculation, reflecting on these concerns of Paul in the light of the letter as a whole could prove productive.

To begin with, the NRSV's translation of the Greek word *ataktoi* as "idlers" is problematic. The word appears only here in the New Testament, although cognates occur at 2 Thessalonians 3:6, 8, and 11. When used of a person, the word generally refers to someone who is undisciplined or insubordinate, as when a soldier is found away from his post. For example, 3 Maccabees 1:19 describes the "disorderly rush" of Jews who gather together in Jerusalem in anticipation of the impending desecration of the temple (see also Josephus, *War* 2:517; *Antiq.* 15:152). The custom of translating *ataktoi* as "idlers" in this passage comes about under the influence of the warnings about idleness in 2 Thessalonians 3:6–13, but there the context makes it clear that the refusal to work is

81

at least part of the problem. Here in 1 Thessalonians 5:14, that is by no means certain, and 2 Thessalonians should not control the translation. A more satisfactory translation would be "disorderly" or "disruptive." To be sure, disorderly or insubordinate behavior within a small community may well result in idleness—a general unwillingness to complete needed tasks or to cooperate with others—but *ataktoi* ought not be limited to this single nuance.

Although such identifications are notoriously risky, scholars often connect these disorderly people with those who are so consumed with enthusiasm for the Parousia and its imminence that they cannot be bothered with staying "in order." Such attitudes may also be at work in the instructions concerning sexual morality in 4:3–8 and the instructions about living quietly and minding one's own affairs in 4:9–12. Those who believe themselves to be waiting for the return of Jesus at any moment may grow impatient with the strictures of an order they understand themselves to have abandoned. Left on their own, these folk may well become wild and wildly offensive in their behavior.

The NRSV's "faint hearted" nicely translates the Greek *oligopsychos,* which literally means "small soul" or "little soul." The word does not appear anywhere else in the New Testament, but it does occur in the Septuagint in the words of encouragement in Isaiah 35:4:

> Say to those who are of a fearful heart [or "faint hearted"],
> "Be strong, do not fear!"

(See also Prov. 18:14; Isa. 54:6; 57:15.) A related noun refers to the anguish of the Israelites under Egyptian captivity (Exod. 6:9). A myriad of causes could produce those who are "faint hearted" among the Thessalonians, the most obvious candidate being the deaths of believers (4:13–18).

The final group to which Paul refers is "the weak." In 1 Corinthians Paul uses the term "weak" of those Christians whose faith is not sufficiently strong to allow them to eat food that has been sacrificed to idols (see, for example, 1 Cor. 8:7–14, and the similar discussion in Romans 14). First Thessalonians offers no evidence that such difficulties plagued the community at Thessalonica, and the term may generally apply to those who are vulnerable to pressures of various sorts. Whether or not this is a real problem in Thessalonica, it certainly worries Paul, who has already expressed his strong concern about the susceptibility of the Thessalonians to the power of "the tempter" (3:5).

82 The disorderly, the faint hearted, and the weak are to be admonished, encouraged, and helped respectively. Concluding this set of terse commands, Paul adds, "Be patient with all of them." Here the

NRSV has inserted the phrase "of them," which does not appear in the Greek, presumably because the context suggests that this exhortation modifies those preceding it and thus refers to these specific groups rather than to all human beings. (Or perhaps the translators simply balk at the prospect of being patient with all?)

Then, as verse 13b ("Be at peace among yourselves") attached a general exhortation to specific concerns for the treatment of the community's leadership, verse 15 concludes the exhortations regarding the treatment of the marginalized in verse 14. The demands that no one should repay "evil for evil" and that good should be sought for all is traditional (see, for example, Prov. 20:22; Matt. 5:38–39, 43; 7:12; Luke 6:27–28; Rom. 12:17; 1 Peter 3:9); however, it takes on a particular nuance in this context. Even if those who are disorderly, discouraged, and weak are not precisely what we would call "evildoers," their behavior tests the limits of a community's tolerance, provoking it to repayment in kind.

If verses 12–13 pose a significant challenge to the contemporary church and its suspicion of anything authoritarian, verses 14–15 challenge our treatment of those who inhabit the margins of our churches. We may not name them as weak, faint hearted, and disorderly, but we do recognize the distressed who sit in the farthest pew and slip out the door without a word to anyone, the susceptible who fall prey to every rumor, the perpetual objection-raisers, faultfinders, problem-pointers. What Paul encourages exceeds the conventions of "making nice" to these people; it is active involvement that seeks their good because their good is that of the whole body of Christ.

The familiarity of Paul's language in this passage could lull contemporary readers into the mistaken assumption that these are simple and straightforward tasks, easily accomplished. But what is more difficult in any group than to be "at peace"? And how hard it is to be patient with the discouraged, the weak, the disorderly—how much easier it is to lose patience and offer them only a flaccid tolerance in place of an earnest effort to "do good to one another and to all." Virtually every congregation and certainly every contemporary denomination offers ample evidence that Paul's instructions constitute a profound challenge to the way things are. Sometimes we are not patient; we are merely indifferent.

Elements of Church Order
(vv. 16–22)

83

The exhortations in verses 16–22 have been the subject of intense discussion. The section consists of a series of brief imperative phrases.

With the exception of verse 18b ("for this is the will of God in Christ Jesus for you") each imperative phrase contains a word, usually the first word, that begins with a "p" sound (from the Greek letter *pi*). The result is a series that might better be presented as follows:

> Rejoice always.
> Pray without ceasing.
> Give thanks in all circumstances (for this is the will of God in Christ Jesus for you).
> Do not quench the Spirit.
> Do not despise the words of prophets.
> But test everything, hold fast to what is good.
> Abstain from every form of evil.

This form as well as the content of these verses have provoked the suggestion that they represent an early form of a church order, such as the one found in the *Didache* (a late first-century Christian writing that instructs believers regarding worship practices and various governance procedures). The first three exhortations in the list (vv. 16–18) clearly belong together. Here Paul recalls the language of the letter's thanksgiving. As the apostles constantly pray for the Thessalonians and give thanks for them, he urges the Thessalonians also to pray and to give thanks. The additional comment, "for this is the will of God in Christ Jesus for you," recalls 4:3; in both places it serves to underscore the importance of the admonitions offered.

All of this seems very familiar, but with "Do not quench the Spirit" readers may feel as if they have wandered into foreign territory. Earlier in the letter, Paul affirms the Spirit's role at Thessalonica (1:5, 6, 7), and it is difficult to imagine what would lead believers to "quench" the work of the Holy Spirit. Help in puzzling this comment out lies in recognizing that all the admonitions in verses 19–22 belong together. Verse 20 ("Do not despise the words of the prophets") explains verse 19; those who reject what is said by the prophets are in danger of attempting to douse the fire of the Holy Spirit. Verses 21–22 offer the constructive alternative to rejection: examine everything carefully, taking hold of the good and leaving the evil alone.

Some scholars have detected in Paul's language the presence of a serious problem at Thessalonica, namely, that wild prophecies regarding the Parousia have prompted the more cautious members of the community to grow suspicious of prophecy altogether. Thomas W. Gillespie concludes that Paul is challenging "the conscious suppression of the Spirit that effects prophecy" (*The First Theologians: A Study in Early Christian Prophecy*, 44).

What is especially important for preachers and teachers is to notice the assumptions Paul's statements reveal. First, Paul assumes that the proper environment for prophecy is *within* the context of the church. That assumption may be deduced from the fact that everything in this section leading up to verses 19–22 addresses believers in their life together—their treatment of leaders and the marginalized, and their prayer life together. The discussion of prophecy in 1 Corinthians 12–14 makes the same assumption, for that entire section of the letter is concerned with matters of corporate worship (11:2—14:40). Paul is concerned not about the occasional rogue prophet who shows up on Sunday morning, spouts off, and leaves town as soon as the dinner dishes have been cleared away (by someone else, assuredly) but about the worship life of the community.

Second, prophecy is a gift of the Spirit of God. Here the connection is implied in the parallel between verse 19 and verse 20. In 1 Corinthians 12:10, he will make the connection explicit. That does not mean that every utterance offered as prophecy is reliable or inspired by the Spirit, but it does mean that prophecy can be genuine and that it comes from the Spirit.

Third, because it can be either true or false, prophecy is not to be rejected out of hand, but neither is it to be accepted uncritically: "test everything; hold fast to what is good, abstain from every form of evil." The words offered as prophecy must not be swallowed whole, but must be subjected to the community for its discernment.

This set of instructions poses a significant challenge to the contemporary church, in which some talk with ease about the working of the Spirit or spiritual direction or spiritual development. Often the terms have about them all the heft of a soap bubble. Others hear any mention of the Spirit as quaint, preferring to subject every decision to extended rational analysis. Paul, as he does with disconcerting regularity, affirms both positions and neither one. The working of the Spirit in the form of prophecy is not to be quenched, but neither is it immune from scrutiny.

A Concluding Prayer
(vv. 23–24)

As in 3:11–13, Paul concludes this section of the letter with a prayer-wish that provides the basis for the admonitions that precede. There is no hope that the Thessalonians can follow Paul's instructions without God's assistance. At the same time, there is every reason to believe that God's assistance will enable them to remain "sound and blameless" at the Parousia.

85

Central to this prayer-wish is the assertion of verse 24, a neglected gem that reveals something crucial about Paul's understanding of the gospel: "The one who calls you is faithful, and he will do this." "The one who calls you" is not vacuous religious verbiage for Paul. Already in this letter he has spoken of the Thessalonians as called (NRSV: "he has chosen you," 1:4; see also 2:12; 4:7). In later letters Paul often refers not only to his own calling as an apostle (Rom. 1:1; 1 Cor. 1:1; Gal. 1:5) but to believers as called by God (Rom. 1:7; 1 Cor. 1:2; Gal. 1:6).

Equally important is the claim that God is faithful. God can be trusted. What Paul takes three chapters to say in Romans 9—11 he articulates here with brilliant concision: God is faithful! This is not a whimsical god who lays traps or plays tricks on humankind simply because she possesses the ability to do so (in the lyrics of *Guys and Dolls*, Lady Luck, who may blow on some other guy's dice). Nor is this one of the fickle gods worshiped in various forms of contemporary religion—career, health, wealth, relationships. This God may be counted on.

The Revised Common Lectionary offers 5:16–24 as an Advent lesson (Year B, Advent 3), which raises several problems. As is often the case with lectionary readings, the lesson begins in the middle of a sense unit. In addition, the connection of the text with Advent is tenuous, since the "coming of our Lord Jesus Christ" refers to his second Advent at the Parousia rather than to the first Advent. The tradition of interpreting the Advent season eschatologically is theologically sound, but it may tax the preacher's skill to make that connection in this passage.

On the other hand, the reading of the ethical exhortations in verses 16–22 in the context of the third Sunday of Advent may prompt some sharp responses. By that advanced stage of December craziness, many will desperately need to hear the words, "Rejoice always" and "give thanks in all circumstances." The promise that God remains faithful despite our frazzled celebration of everything but the birth of the infant son of God could prove to be particularly timely.

During another season of the year, a sermon on this passage might well explore the church's responsibilities to those in its midst as leaders and those on its margins who are deeply troubled. Paul's words about prophecy also prompt reflection on the ways in which we seek either to avoid the work of the Spirit or to avoid subjecting it to critical scrutiny.

Read This Letter!

1 THESSALONIANS 5:25–28

Following the prayer-wish in verses 23–24, with its powerful reminder about God's fidelity and power, Paul brings the letter to a close with elements that will become standard in his letters: a request for prayer (Rom. 15:30; Philemon 22), greetings to members of the congregation (Rom. 16:1–16, 21–23; 1 Cor. 16:19; 2 Cor. 13:12; Phil. 4:21–22; Philemon 15), instructions to share in a holy kiss (1 Cor. 16:20; 2 Cor. 13:12), and the invocation of grace upon the recipients of the letter (Rom. 16:20; 1 Cor. 16:23; 2 Cor. 13:13; Gal. 6:18; Phil. 4:23; Philemon 15).

One element in this closing does come as a surprise, for no other letter demands the public reading of the letter. (Colossians 4:16 gives instructions about when the letter is read, but that passage differs sharply from 1 Thess. 5:27; in addition, Colossians was probably written by a member of the Pauline school rather than by Paul himself.) Paul's choice of words here is astonishingly sharp. The Greek verb he uses (*enorkizein*) appears nowhere else in the New Testament and only rarely outside. A related verb that is *less* emphatic (*orkizein*) appears in Mark 5:7 and Acts 19:13 for the casting out of demons, raising the troublesome question of why Paul resorts to such extreme language. In other letters, we might suppose that he is aware of factions in the church and speaks harshly because he fears that some will not be told of the arrival of his letter. First Thessalonians contains little indication of factions, however, and it may be that Paul was self-consciously insisting that the community take seriously the letter he has written as a communication *to the community;* that is, it is a positive theological claim about the character of his letter rather than a strategy for plastering over the cracks that are beginning to etch their fine lace into the walls.

Perhaps Paul wanted the letter to be read in the context of worship, although we need not think of this as a formal gathering. One conventional way of publishing a text in the ancient world was to gather a group of friends who would read the work and then engage one another in a discussion. In some respects, the process resembles publishing on modern computer networks, where there is no commercial selling and buying and where responses can change the nature of the text. By virtue of reading the letter in the context of the community, the Thessalonians put the letter "on-line," where it has remained ever since.

As with the opening salutation, it is difficult to imagine that many pastors would preach on the closing lines of a letter, yet Paul says much here about the nature of the church, especially if we read the closing lines in light of the letter as a whole. The poignant request that the brothers and sisters in Thessalonica pray for the apostle and the instructions to greet one another with a kiss reiterate the powerful relationship that has been forged at Thessalonica and between the Thessalonians and the apostles. The closing invocation of the grace of Jesus Christ places that relationship in its only proper context, that of God's action in Jesus Christ. This is a community characterized by a profound sense of connection, but created by the grace of God in Jesus Christ. To omit either of those features is to misconstrue the nature of the gospel in a fundamental way.

Teachers who have worked through this letter with a group may now find it especially helpful to read the letter aloud (or have it read) all the way through in a class setting. Participants could be invited to reflect on the responses the Thessalonians might have made to Paul's letter. What might they suggest adding, changing, restating, deleting? And what responses does the letter elicit today?

Second Thessalonians

Introduction

The congregation at Pilgrim's Rest Church had been listening to Reverend Lawson's sermons for eight years when she surprised them last Sunday with something unlike her usual fare. Most Sundays she makes at least one reference to the life of John Wesley and the need for moral growth. She always preaches from one of the assigned lectionary passages, but she works in quotations from Matthew, her favorite Gospel, as often as possible. A musical group from the 1960s frequently makes an appearance before the sermon is finished.

Last Sunday the sermon took off in an altogether different direction. The New Testament reading was from Romans, but the sermon made so little reference to the Bible that it was hard to remember what the lesson had been without looking at the Order of Service. Most of what Reverend Lawson said came from her reading of someone named Karl Barth. And, instead of talking about struggling toward perfection, she rambled on and on about the greatness of God and God's unmerited grace toward humankind. The sermon concluded with a quotation from John Donne.

Few people in worship that morning paid much attention to the difference, but those who did were exceedingly curious. Over coffee during the following week, they wondered aloud what prompted the sudden change. One hoped Reverend Lawson had finally run out of stories about John Wesley. Another was relieved to hear her talk about God. But one person dared to suggest that perhaps Reverend Lawson had not actually written that new sermon herself; she had simply

89

borrowed it from another preacher elsewhere, or maybe from a magazine for preachers. Whatever the explanation, this new sermon startled careful listeners and provoked more than a little curiosity.

Second Thessalonians presents readers of the letters of Paul with a puzzle similar to that facing the congregation at Pilgrim's Rest: How do we understand this letter, which claims to be from Paul but which differs strikingly from his other letters and especially from 1 Thessalonians? To be sure, far more important questions arise about this letter, questions having to do with its content and its value for the church. The question of authorship persists, however, and by exploring it we pay close attention to the content, which positions us to consider the value of the letter. In other words, the authorship question is not the preserve of antiquarians but a way of asking about the content and contribution of the letter.

The Structure of the Letter:
1 Thessalonians Recalled

One feature of 2 Thessalonians that prompts curiosity is that its structure closely resembles that of 1 Thessalonians. General resemblance is taken for granted, of course, since the New Testament letters follow the letter-writing conventions of the day; here, however, the resemblance extends beyond matters of form (salutation, closing greetings, and so forth) to subject matter and even wording.

The following analysis of the structure of 2 Thessalonians provides an overview:

Salutation	1:1–2
Thanksgiving	1:3–12
Body	2:1–17
Day of the Lord	2:1–12
Concluding Thanksgiving and Prayer	2:13–17
Ethical Instruction	3:1–15
Concerning Prayer for the Apostles	3:1–5
Concerning Idleness	3:6–13
Concerning the Disobedient	3:14–15
Closing	3:16–18

Like 1 Thessalonians, this letter includes an extended thanksgiving that mentions the faith and love of the Thessalonians and their response to persecution (1:3–12; cf. 1 Thess. 1:2–10). The body of each letter contains a prayer of thanksgiving (1 Thess. 2:13 and 2 Thess. 2:13) and concludes with a prayer-wish (1 Thess. 3:11–13 and 2 Thess. 2:16–17). Both letters contain the same elements of closing in the same order.

90

The similarities extend to matters of wording. The salutations are nearly identical, apart from the use of *"our* Father" in 2 Thessalonians rather than *"the* Father" in 1 Thessalonians and the repetition of the phrase "from God our Father and the Lord Jesus Christ" in 2 Thessalonians 1:2. Second Thessalonians 3:8 ("with toil and labor we worked night and day, so that we might not burden any of you") closely follows the wording of 1 Thessalonians 2:9. The prayer-wish concluding the body of each letter calls on God to "strengthen" the hearts of the Thessalonians (1 Thess. 3:13; 2 Thess. 2:17), an expression not found elsewhere in Paul.

More detailed comparisons of the two letters are available elsewhere (Edgar Krentz provides a helpful summary in "First and Second Epistles to the Thessalonians"), but these examples will suffice to identify the problem facing readers: 2 Thessalonians closely follows the form and language of 1 Thessalonians. Do these similarities mean that Paul wrote a second letter rather soon after the first and so unconsciously repeated himself, or do they suggest imitation of 1 Thessalonians by a later writer?

**The Content of the Letter:
1 Thessalonians Rejected?**

Over against the similarities between the two letters, the content of 2 Thessalonians differs markedly from that of 1 Thessalonians. The major concerns of 1 Thessalonians have diminished or disappeared in this letter, and minor concerns in 1 Thessalonians have increased in volume and intensity.

One of the major issues in 1 Thessalonians is that of the close relationship between the apostles and the Thessalonians. It virtually dominates 1 Thessalonians 1 and 2, yet it disappears when we turn to 2 Thessalonians. Paul continues to address the Thessalonians as "brothers and sisters" (1:3; 2:1, 13, 15; 3:1, 13), and at 3:1 he asks the Thessalonians to pray for the apostles in their work of spreading the gospel. Yet the other familial imagery of 1 Thessalonians has disappeared—the warm descriptions of the apostles as fathers, nurses, mothers, and orphans. In addition, although such judgments are highly subjective, here we find little of the affect of 1 Thessalonians. Nothing resembles 1 Thessalonians 2:17—3:5, with its deep concern for these new believers and longing for reunion with them.

A second major concern in 1 Thessalonians is that of the community of believers. Paul warns believers against sexual practices that would do harm to fellow believers (1 Thess. 4:6), urges believers to encourage one another (1 Thess. 4:18; 5:11), and includes several specific

91

admonitions about life within the community (1 Thess. 5:12–22). Such concern for the quality of community life is strikingly absent from 2 Thessalonians. The thanksgiving celebrates the fact that the community is increasing in its love (2 Thess. 1:3), but the letter itself says nothing more on this topic. Even in 3:6–13, where the warning against idleness might well claim that idleness harms the other members of the community (see 1 Thess. 4:9–12), nothing is said to indicate that the community as such is a cause for concern.

Another major concern that dominates 1 Thessalonians, especially in chapters 4 and 5, is ethics. In particular, Paul seems concerned to offer an ethic that will set believers apart from the Gentile world; hence the concern for sexual morality and the behavior of believers to one another. Second Thessalonians also demonstrates a concern with ethics, but here the focus has narrowed sharply from that of 1 Thessalonians. Primarily it is confined to the single issue of idleness (2 Thess. 3:6–13).

One major concern of 1 Thessalonians that does reappear in 2 Thessalonians is that of eschatology, and here it even dominates the letter. More important, and indeed central to the discussion of the authorship question, is that what this letter asserts about the eschaton seems sharply at odds with the comments of 1 Thessalonians. Although 1 Thessalonians looks forward to the return of Jesus in the near future (1 Thess. 4:15; 5:10), 2 Thessalonians warns against those who claim that the "day of the Lord" has already arrived (2 Thess. 2:2). And although 1 Thessalonians hints that no one knows how to predict the arrival of that day (1 Thess. 5:2–3), 2 Thessalonians narrates the signs that must precede it (2 Thess. 2:3–8).

Closely related to the eschatological content of 2 Thessalonians is its treatment of persecution and the future judgment. In 1 Thessalonians, these issues play only a minor role. Paul refers to the sufferings endured by the apostles and the Thessalonians (1:6; 2:14; 3:3), as well as by believers in Judea (2:14). He also makes indirect reference to a final judgment (1:10; 3:13; 5:2–10). In 2 Thessalonians, however, these concerns move to the center in very harsh terms. The thanksgiving introduces those who persecute believers (1:4, 6); presumably that persecution itself anticipates the final days of rebellion and lawlessness (2:3–12). There are "wicked and evil" people from whom believers must be protected (3:2–3). Not content with reminding the audience of God's ability to rescue believers from evil, the letter revels in the coming heavenly judgment against all who "do not know God" and who "do not obey the gospel" (1:8); such people will receive an eternal punishment "separated from the presence of the Lord and from the glory of his might" (1:9). The promise of this letter is that God's judgment is certain and sure; the tone that pervades the letter is rage.

Unlike 1 Thessalonians, scholars agree that the rhetorical purpose of 2 Thessalonians is clear. The letter is an example of deliberative rhetoric, in that it urges the recipients to adopt (and maintain) a particular course of action in the future. The Thessalonians are to continue steadfast, faithful to the traditions given them by the apostles and observant of the letter's warnings about idleness and disobedience.

**The Question of
Authorship and Audience**

This brief comparison of the two letters sharpens the question of authorship: How do we account for this curious combination of *similarities* in the structure and language of these letters, on the one hand, and the *differences* in content and tone, on the other?

Answers to this question divide scholars. Until the late eighteenth century, scholars assumed that the letter was written by the same Paul who wrote 1 Thessalonians, and some scholars maintain that viewpoint at present. They point to the fact that 2 Thessalonians appears in early Christian versions of the canon and that other Christian writers quote it early in the second century; thus, the evidence for its existence is as strong and early as that of the other Pauline letters. On this view, the similarities in structure and language occur because Paul writes this second letter only a few months after the first. Although there are several explanations, one common view is that the situation at Thessalonica has deteriorated in a short period of time. Persecution has become more intense, and in its wake apocalyptic frenzy has led both to the unwillingness to work and to wild speculation about the return of Jesus.

An increasing number of scholars, myself included, find themselves unable to reconcile 2 Thessalonians with 1 Thessalonians and, indeed, with the remainder of the Pauline letter corpus. In addition to the problems already noted, these scholars see the reference to forgery in 2:2 as problematic; if only a few months separated the writing of the two letters, it is difficult to understand how spurious letters were written and circulated in the interim. Perhaps more difficult is the strong assertion in 3:17: "I, Paul, write this greeting with my own hand. This is the mark *in every letter of mine; it is the way I write*" (emphasis added). Although Paul does often conclude his letters in his own handwriting (e.g., Gal 6:11; 1 Cor. 16:21; Philemon 19), nowhere else do we find the explicit assertion that this is the way he routinely writes. In addition, if 1 Thessalonians is Paul's first letter and 2 Thessalonians follows closely on it, then what does Paul mean by "every letter of mine"?

93

On this theory, a later Christian, perhaps one from the circle of Paul's coworkers or students, called on the authority of Paul to speak to a situation of intense persecution. Looking into the face of powerful enemies, that individual rages that God will finally require an accounting of those who torment the faithful. The letter itself contains no hint as to its date, but persecution did grow more pronounced in certain locations toward the end of the first century, so that a late first-century date is reasonable. That would make it possible for the letter to be cited by early second-century writers. The location of writing and identity of the audience are impossible to determine; that the writer addresses "Thessalonians" means only that he is drawing on the authority of an earlier letter to Christians in that city.

The question of authorship has so dominated scholarly discussion of 2 Thessalonians in recent decades that it threatens to make every commentary on the letter into a volley fired into the battle over authorship. Having introduced some of the problems here, the commentary will attempt to avoid that difficulty by attending to the letter itself, with little reference to the question of authorship. It will refer to "the writer" or "2 Thessalonians" instead of Paul and to "the audience" or "the readers" instead of the Thessalonians. In this way perhaps both readers who affirm and those who question Pauline authorship will find the commentary itself valuable and will not find the authorship debate distracting.

The Nuclear Holocaust Response

The suggestion that Paul may not have written 2 Thessalonians sometimes elicits an immediate, and immediately negative, protest: "But the letter begins with 'Paul, Silvanus, and Timothy,' and it ends with 'I, Paul, write this greeting with my own hand.' How can anyone say Paul did not write it? If he did not, then the Bible contains a lie. And if it contains one lie, how can I trust anything in it?"

This response somewhat resembles what high school debaters call the "nuclear holocaust" strategy. The debater tries to destroy the position of the opposing team by arguing that it will lead to dire consequences, the end result of which is the inevitable annihilation of the planet Earth and all its inhabitants. Most Christian lay people are not self-consciously employing the "nuclear holocaust" strategy in order to triumph over the teacher or preacher as in a debate; their reaction is utterly sincere. In their view, if "Paul, Silvanus, and Timothy" are not the authors of 2 Thessalonians, then 2 Thessalonians contains a lie, a lie that undermines the truth claims of Scripture as a whole.

And, indeed, if Reverend Lawson did "borrow" her sermon on Romans from another preacher rather than doing her own work, she would be guilty of plagiarism and her work would be discredited. The same standard would appear to dictate that a writer who attached Paul's name to his own letter was guilty of fraud. In the ancient world, however, the writing of a letter under the name of another person did not necessarily constitute gross intellectual fraud. To be sure, there were individuals who wrote under an assumed name in order to sell that work and make a profit; such a motive is scarcely imaginable for the writing of 2 Thessalonians, since its sales expectations would be nonexistent. More to the point, disciples or followers of a revered figure could write in the name of that individual in order to address a new situation in terms that would be pertinent and meaningful. In other words, by the standards of the first century, what the author of 2 Thessalonians does reveals esteem for Paul and would not be regarded as disrespectful.

Discussion of pseudepigraphy has little, if any, place in the pulpit, but it does belong in the church's educational program. It is one of a network of issues that make contemporary readers aware that their expectations and values differ at points from those of ancient readers. Ironically, although we daily learn ways in which our cultural norms differ from those of people who may live only blocks away, we still expect that the Bible will mirror our own culture and its ways. Perhaps more important, pastors who will frankly acknowledge the question of pseudepigraphy (whatever their own final judgments on the question) may find that they allow other readers to voice long-suppressed questions of their own, thereby opening doors to a teachable moment.

A Difficult Letter
and the Question of Significance

As controversial as the question of authorship is for some readers of 2 Thessalonians, the more challenging question is what significance this letter has for the life of the church two millennia after its composition. Second Thessalonians plainly reflects an atmosphere in which believers are experiencing persecution. The situation has become so intense that some believers cope with it by imagining that the "day of the Lord is already here" (2:2), while others refuse to participate in the world of work (3:6–13). The author probably imagines that his enraged reminders about God's inevitable justice will serve to comfort his audience; however, those same reminders sound a harsh note for readers removed from 2 Thessalonians in time and situation.

The commentary that follows candidly acknowledges that 2 Thessalonians is a challenging letter. It forces the hard question of how to preach and teach passages we find difficult. First, the simple act of admitting the

95

difficulties may be freeing to us and to those who hear us. Admitting our puzzlement is preferable to covering over things. (The Revised Common Lectionary appears to do just that by the way it selectively avoids certain passages in this letter.)

Second, we still need to ask what this text has to say, whether we are prepared to hear it or not. Part of the reason we find 2 Thessalonians difficult is that it raises issues that make us terribly uncomfortable. It may be that we need to hear those issues, precisely because they are challenges we refuse to face, issues we would prefer not to have to address.

The commentary will explore some of those issues at close range, but it may be helpful to identify a few of them before turning to the letter itself:

First, 2 Thessalonians starkly portrays the persistence of evil in the world created and sustained by God. Evil exists in the behavior of those human beings who persecute believers (1:4, 6–7) and reject the gospel of Jesus Christ (1:8; 3:2). More powerfully, it exists in those greater-than-human forces of rebellion and lawlessness. In order to depict this evil, the author narrates a small story in which lawlessness and rebellion are personified (2:3–12). This raises the disturbing question of whether we sufficiently acknowledge the reality of evil in the world (see "Reflection: The Persistence of Evil," pp. 118–120 below).

Second, in the face of the persistence of evil, 2 Thessalonians insists that God is a God of justice. This is, of course, hardly the only biblical witness to make such an assertion, but the dominance of the claim in this brief letter makes it noteworthy. As Edgar Krentz has observed, here God's "fundamental character" is justice; God demonstrates justice both when God "repays the persecutors of his assembly with persecution" and when God grants the afflicted respite from their suffering ("Through a Lens: Theology and Fidelity in 2 Thessalonians," 58). Since the author's remarks address believers rather than their oppressors, their purpose is to comfort the afflicted rather than to chasten the afflictors.

Third, denouncing evil and calling on the God of justice, 2 Thessalonians rages. Donald H. Juel has urged that we recover the reading of Scripture aloud, attending to the ways in which the oral reading of a passage embodies the interpretation that has been chosen ("The Strange Silence of the Bible"). Following that lead, it is intriguing to ask whether we can read 2 Thessalonians 2 quietly, or 2 Thessalonians 1. Whatever the volume, to do justice to such texts requires the tremulous voice of rage. What might such rage have to say to those Christians who have been taught that "nice" people, true Christians, do not allow themselves to become angry? Does 2 Thessalonians place before us the obligation to rage against evil?

96

Fourth, the turbulence that characterizes these first three issues stands bracketed by the letter's claims about peace. Second Thessalonians opens with a greeting of "grace and peace from God our Father and the Lord Jesus Christ." It closes with a prayer that "the Lord of peace himself" might grant believers "peace at all times in all ways." One challenge the letter presents is to consider what it means to affirm the peacefulness of God and the peace granted by God, while simultaneously affirming the ongoing presence of evil in the world and the inescapability of God's justice. What kind of peace does 2 Thessalonians envision and how might it instruct believers in the present?

Second Thessalonians will continue to trouble preachers and teachers. Few would argue that this letter is pivotal for understanding the New Testament. Yet the harsh, even ominous language that characterizes this text troubles us precisely because it raises significant issues that the church all too often prefers to neglect.

Commentary on Second Thessalonians

The opening verses of 2 Thessalonians closely resemble those of 1 Thessalonians. By the end of the thanksgiving, however, the reader knows that the problem of persecution presses on the readers of this letter. The remainder of the first chapter, and indeed much of the letter, concern the writer's anticipation of the judgment that is to come on those who persecute the community and the corresponding reward of the faithful. The atmosphere is thick and heavy; gone is the joy of 1 Thessalonians, its place occupied by the language of vengeance and concern for the response to persecution.

The problem for readers of this letter in a modern context, particularly a North American context, emerges rather quickly in these opening verses: How do we read this letter with its relentless promise of salvation for persecuted believers and damnation for their adversaries in the setting of a church that is dwindling and distressed but seldom persecuted? Who needs to persecute such a church, which itself threatens no one and nothing? That is not to deny that the church in North America faces threats, but most are threats that might better be characterized as indifference and self-preoccupation rather than as dangers imposed from external enemies. None of this argues for placing brackets around 2 Thessalonians, but it may mean that we will not readily find ourselves in situations analogous to those of the readers of this letter; instead, we need to ask how the letter challenges and instructs a very different contemporary Christianity.

97

Grace to You and Peace

2 THESSALONIANS 1:1–2

The opening salutation (vv. 1–2) is virtually identical to the opening of 1 Thessalonians (see above on 1 Thess. 1:1). The two alterations only serve to make explicit in 2 Thessalonians what is implicit in 1 Thessalonians. Here the writer identifies God as "our" Father in verse 1 and adds "from God our Father and the Lord Jesus Christ" to the "grace and peace" (v. 2). By making those statements explicit, however, verses 1 and 2 become repetitious in that each of them ends with the identical phrase, "God our Father and the Lord Jesus Christ." As is the case throughout the letters, and indeed throughout the New Testament, the wording assumes that the church has its rightful location in God (see above on 1 Thess. 1:1). That reminder plays an important role in this letter, for if the church is God's own, then its enemies are also God's enemies.

In the context of the letter that follows, the language of peace in verse 2 is jarring. With its threats of vengeance and eternal destruction and lawlessness and delusion, 2 Thessalonians sounds anything but peaceful. Yet the letter both begins and ends (see 3:16) with words of peace. This may be the result of the author's conscious imitation of the Pauline letters, in which invocations of peace regularly appear (Rom. 1:7; 1 Cor. 1:3; 2 Cor. 1:2; Gal. 1:3; Phil. 1:2; Philemon 1:3). Jouette Bassler has argued, however, that a key feature of 2 Thessalonians is the assurance of peace *for the believing community*, which means that framing the letter with talk of peace is no mere formality but provides a lens through which to read the letter ("Peace in All Ways: Theology in the Thessalonian Letters," 76–81).

Thanksgiving and Judgment

2 THESSALONIANS 1:3–12

The thanksgiving begins in verse 3 and extends, formally, through verse 12. Despite the paragraph division in the NRSV (and the RSV and NAB, but note the REB) verse 5 cannot be separated sharply from verse 4. In fact, all of verses 3–10 constitutes one long sentence in Greek. And "to this end" (Gr. *eis ho*), which introduces verses 11–12, directly links those verses back to verses 3–10.

This long thanksgiving comprises three distinct sections, despite these grammatical links among them. Verses 3–4 identify the main topics of thanksgiving. Their reference to the "persecutions and afflictions" being experienced by the Thessalonians prompts an elaboration on the eventual outcome of those sufferings in verses 5–10. The thanksgiving concludes in verses 11–12 with a prayer for the continued faith (or faithfulness) of the Thessalonians.

The Duty of Thanksgiving (vv. 3–4)

The words that introduce the thanksgiving have prompted scholarly interest: "We must always give thanks to God for you, brothers and sisters, as is right." This reference to obligation has caused some scholars who affirm the Pauline authorship of this letter to assume that, in the interval between the writing of 1 and 2 Thessalonians, the Thessalonians have protested their unworthiness of the extended thanksgiving in the first letter. In response, Paul insists on the necessity of thanksgiving. And scholars who deny Pauline authorship sometimes detect in the "We must" and "as is right" an emotional "coolness" or distance uncharacteristic of Paul. Roger Aus rightly notes, by contrast with both these arguments, that the obligation of human beings to give thanks to God is a motif in both Jewish and Christian writings in this period ("The Liturgical Background of the Necessity and Propriety of Giving Thanks according to 2 Thes 1:3"). For example, the Jewish writer Philo insists that "it is meet and right that the hospitality of God should be praised and revered, God who provides for His guests the whole earth as a truly hospitable home ever filled not merely with necessaries, but with the means of luxurious living" (*Special Laws* 2.173; see also 1.224; 2.185; *Allegorical Interpretation* 3:10). And the Christian epistle of *Barnabas* claims that "we should know him to whom we ought to give thanks and praise for everything" (7.1; see also 5.3 and *1 Clement* 38.4). In other words, the writer is simply acknowledging, as do others of his era, the need for gratitude to God in light of God's role as creator and sustainer of life (see also 2:13).

The thanksgiving offered here quickly becomes specific: "your faith is growing abundantly, and the love of everyone of you for one another is increasing" (v. 3). Given the importance in 1 Thessalonians of the "faith, love, and hope" triad (1:3; 3:6; and see, of course, 1 Cor. 13:13), the absence of hope here is striking. Unlike 1 Thessalonians,

99

which frequently speaks of hope, particularly the hope of the Parousia (1:3; 2:19; 4:13; 5:8), in this letter the word appears only in 2:16, and there it does not refer to the Parousia.

Given the fact that we generally equate faith with belief or trust, perhaps most often belief in a certain set of propositions or a body of information, we may naturally understand the writer's assertion that the Thessalonians are "growing abundantly" in their faith as a claim about the strength of their convictions—faith as distinct from doubt. Already in 1 Thessalonians, however, faith is described as "your work of faith" (1:3), implying that faith has an active quality that manifests itself in concrete labor. More important, in verse 4 faith almost certainly means faithfulness or endurance in the face of suffering. That might suggest that the nuance in verse 3 is also faithfulness (and see similar connotations of faith [Gr. *pistis*] in Rom. 3:3; Gal. 5:22; Titus 2:10).

The writer also gives thanks for the love within the community and does so with an unusual expression: "the love of everyone of you for one another is increasing." First Thessalonians 3:12 also refers to mutual love with the expression "love for one another and for all" (see also Phil. 1:9), but here the language becomes a shade more emphatic with "the love of *everyone* of you for one another," an expression that is without parallel in the New Testament. This insistence on everyone's participation may anticipate the sharp division the letter makes between those within the community, who are presently suffering and who will welcome the glorious return of Jesus, and those on the outside who are persecuting the community and who will eventually be punished by eternal separation from God. In addition, the "everyone" may seek to include those among the Thessalonians who are not following the traditions and practices taught by the apostles (see 3:6–15). With the word "everyone," the writer builds a fence around the community, bringing in those who may be straying to the perimeter and shutting out those who are perceived as a threat.

By giving thanks for the faith (or faithfulness) and strong mutual love within this community, verse 3 lays the groundwork for the writer's "boast" in verse 4. The Thessalonians deserve boasting for a very particular set of reasons that has to do with their context of persecutions and afflictions. Here the writer repeats the observation of the community's "faith" and adds to that the powerful term, "steadfastness" (Gr. *hypomonē*). Perhaps best thought of as that dogged determination that will not let go, no matter how contrary the circumstances, "steadfastness," or "endurance" as it is often translated, is associated in the New Testament with persecution (see, for example, Luke 21:29; Rom. 5:3–4; 2 Cor. 6:4; Rev. 1:9; 13:10) or with the anticipation of the eschaton (Rom. 8:25; 1 Thess. 1:3).

As noted in the discussion of 1 Thessalonians, the thanksgivings in the Pauline letters routinely offer readers clues as to the issues that will dominate the letter to follow. In this letter, that issue becomes clear in verse 4, the real "table of contents": "your steadfastness and faith during all your persecutions and the afflictions that you are enduring." What these "persecutions and afflictions" are—physical harm, social ostracism, economic pressure—the letter gives us no clue. As is the case in many New Testament texts, the references to persecution assume that the readers will know what circumstances are in view. We twentieth-century readers do not have that information, however, and are unlikely to gain it.

If we do not know what these "persecutions and afflictions" (Gr. *diōgmos* and *thlipsis*) are, we do know the language itself from elsewhere in the New Testament and the Septuagint. For example, Daniel 12:1 contemplates anguish (Gr. *thlipsis*) "such as has never occurred since nations first came into existence." Zephaniah 1:15 anticipates the "day of the Lord" as "a day of distress and anguish" (see also Nahum 1:7; Obad. 12–14; Hab. 3:16). In the New Testament, these terms refer to the struggles inevitably experienced by believers (see, for example, Mark 4:17; John 16:33; Acts 14:22; Phil. 1:17) and are often interpreted as signs of the impending eschaton (Mark 13:19, 24; Rev. 7:14). Precisely because of the association between persecution and the Parousia, it is necessary to explain what these events mean and how they are related to the Parousia of Jesus Christ (see 1:5—2:12).

One additional feature of this verse merits our attention, and that is the writer's claim that he boasts of the Thessalonians "among the churches of God." As noted in the discussion of 1 Thessalonians 2:19, Paul sometimes speaks of his pride in the churches in an eschatological sense; that is, he will present them before God as evidence of his own faithfulness. Here it is before the churches themselves that a boast is made (see also 2 Cor. 7:4, 14; 8:24; 9:3). What churches these were and what their circumstances we can only imagine. If the writer is not Paul but a later figure employing Paul's name and authority to speak to a new generation, then there may be no real context for boasting. This may be a rhetorical strategy. Instead, these words become a boast to the church in every era and, indeed, to our churches in our time. The writer's boast about this group of unknown Christians in circumstances of trial and danger calls contemporary Christians to thanksgiving for the faithfulness and steadfastness of all those who made our own faith possible.

The details of verses 3–4 provide important clues for reading the letter ahead, but those details should not obscure the fact that we are in the midst of a period of thanksgiving. The writer renders thanks to

God for the Thessalonians, for their growing faith and love. However much it is appropriate to boast on their account, it is appropriate only because it is God who has made this growth and endurance possible. The import of this apparently benign assertion emerges when we consider the temptation to celebrate church growth as an "achievement" rather than a gift (and that other temptation—to find a scapegoat when there is no growth to celebrate). For the writer of 2 Thessalonians, the thanksgiving belongs only to God.

The Fierce and Final Judgment (vv. 5–10)

The preoccupation of 2 Thessalonians, however, quickly turns in verse 5 to God's justice: "This is evidence of the righteous judgment of God. . . . " Although, as noted above, verses 3–10 comprise one long sentence in the Greek, the nature of the grammatical relationship between verse 4 and verse 5 is obscure, so that the antecedent of "evidence" is unspecified. The resulting challenge for interpretation is apparent in the NRSV: What exactly is it that the writer regards as "evidence" of God's judgment? Is it the general situation described in verses 3–4, the steadfastness of the Thessalonians under persecution, or the persecutions and afflictions themselves?

Some scholars have suggested that at this point 2 Thessalonians is influenced by a theology of suffering that can be discerned in Jewish literature of this period. One example often pointed to is 2 Maccabees. Written in the late second century B.C.E., 2 Maccabees struggles to explain the severe persecution of Jews under the reign of Antiochus Epiphanes and concludes that God permits the faithful to be punished immediately for their sins but will allow others to continue in sin until they have achieved "the full measure" before punishing them (2 Macc. 6:12–17). The writer of the *Psalms of Solomon* (first century B.C.E.) contrasts the fate of the godless with that of the righteous person:

> For the Lord will spare his devout,
>   and he will wipe away their mistakes with discipline.
> For the life of the righteous (goes on) forever,
>   but sinners shall be taken away to destruction,
>   and no memory of them will ever be found.
>   (*Pss. Sol.* 13:9–10)

102 For these writers and others (see, for example, *2 Baruch* 13:3–10; 48:48–50; 52:5–7) God's justice is unfailing and demands retribution for sins committed. Those who are faithful in this life may expect to be

rewarded after death, but they experience suffering in the present to pay for their (relatively few) sins and to prepare them for their glorious future. Those who are not faithful in this life will experience severe punishment in the future. Our passage does not conform to this pattern entirely, since the writer says nothing about the few sins of the good that need to be expiated. Instead of being retribution for sins, the sufferings presently undergone by the good have the function of rendering them "worthy of the kingdom of God."

Pastors will not need to be told of the dangers that lurk in statements such as this one. The medicine that offers comfort and sustenance to one generation can readily become the horse pill that chokes the next, with words such as "You just remember that God intends this tragedy of yours for the good." The logical pratfalls attendant on such a scheme are astounding: Shall I measure my standing with God by my misfortunes (since God is punishing me now and will reward me later)? If I find myself at relative ease, does that mean that I can anticipate great anguish after death? Explanations intended to strengthen the beleaguered do not necessarily translate well into systematic theology.

Whatever the precise move between verses 4 and 5, with verse 6 it becomes clear that the author's concern is to comfort the church with the promise that those who afflict it will meet with justice. Here the reasoning begins with a fundamental assertion of biblical tradition, that God's justice is reliable and trustworthy. That claim is not argued but assumed, and the energy of the passage moves confidently toward the promise that God's justice is inescapable: the time of reckoning *is* ahead.

Second Thessalonians conjures a future for the persecutors in the harshest of imagery. God will "repay with affliction those who afflict you" (v. 7). Notice, however, that verse 8 extends this circle of punishment to include "those who do not know God" and "those who do not obey the gospel of our Lord Jesus." Elsewhere in the Bible, "those who do not know God" is a conventional expression for Gentiles, as in 1 Thessalonians 4:5 (see also Rom. 1:21), Psalms 79:6, and Jeremiah 10:25. The next expression, "those who do not obey the gospel of our Lord Jesus," is far from conventional; the closest parallel appears in Romans 10:16 in reference to Jews ("not all have obeyed the good news"). There it is clearly synonymous with belief in Jesus, but in 2 Thessalonians obedience later becomes quite specific (see 3:14), so that it is unclear whether this expression refers to unbelievers (perhaps unbelieving Jews, as the complement to the Gentiles who "do not know God") or to apostate Christians.

Even more confusing is the question of the relationship between the people identified in verse 8 and the afflictors of the faithful (v. 6).

103

If the disobedient are apostate Christians, it is understandable that the writer might identify them with the church's persecutors. Surely, however, even in his outrage, the writer does not think that all who "do not know God" are persecutors of the church. Rhetoric has triumphed over logic.

For all these groups, at the Parousia there will be vengeance. Verse 9 imagines that vengeance in terrifying terms, as "eternal destruction, separated from the presence of the Lord and from the glory of his might." The language about God's presence recalls that of Isaiah 2:10 (see also 2:19, 21; cf. Isa. 66; Obad. 15–16):

> Enter into the rock,
>   and hide in the dust
> from the terror of the Lord
>   and from the glory of his majesty.

By contrast with 1 Thessalonians 4:17 and 5:10, which promise believers that they will live in the presence of the Lord always, 2 Thessalonians offers persecutors the promise of forever being banished from that same presence (cf. Matt. 25:41: "Depart from me").

Unlike the awesome description of the fate of the afflictors, the writer gives little attention to the future of believers. He characterizes it with the single word "relief" or "rest" (Gr. *anesis*). Beyond that single word, the return of Jesus itself *is* the future of believers. They will marvel at Jesus' revelation (v. 9); his name will be glorified in them, and they will be glorified in him (v. 12). If, as some think, this group is overly preoccupied with the eschaton, even to the extent of proclaiming in its own troubles the eschatological sufferings and seeing the day of the Lord as already come, then the unwillingness to speak about the future of believers in detail may be strategic.

The "picture" verses 7–8 create of this revelation is so attenuated that it verges on the comical. (Is it Jesus or his angels who are "in flaming fire," and is this a version of an apocalyptic flambé?) Of course, the writer telegraphs through these brief references the character of the event anticipated. The accompaniment of angels or other heavenly beings signals the arrival of the divine (see, for example, 1 Thess. 4:16; Mark 13:26; Rev. 19:17; Isa. 13:2–5). Similarly, fire is regularly associated with theophanies (Exod. 3:2; Deut. 33:2; Acts 7:30) and with apocalyptic scenarios of judgment (Isa. 66:15–16; Dan. 7:9–10).

However much the language here shares with such passages as 1 Corinthians 15 and 1 Thessalonians 4, the tenor differs slightly from those two Pauline texts. First Corinthians 15 anticipates the return of Jesus as the guarantor of God's power, for the Parousia culminates the

104

power play of the resurrection. And 1 Thessalonians 4 promises that Jesus' return will bring comfort to believers, who will be united with him and with those believers who have died. Here, however, Jesus comes as the awesome, eschatological judge, the one who wreaks vengeance on the church's enemies by banishing them eternally and revealing his own glory.

In verses 5–10 the wrath to be inflicted on the persecutors of God's people and those who reject the gospel has threatened to eclipse the community to which the writer speaks. In verses 11–12, however, they appear again in the context of a prayer that they may be made worthy and that they might be glorified along with the name of the Lord Jesus. On first reading, verse 12 seems painfully convoluted, with the "name of our Lord Jesus" being glorified "according to the grace of our God and the Lord Jesus Christ." A shrewd editor would insist on tidying up the prose here, excising one reference to the "Lord Jesus" and probably the whole of the "according to" phrase. The repetition serves an important function, however, by insisting once again that only grace makes it possible for human beings to give glory to God and only grace can imagine something remotely related to human glory.

Proclaiming Judgment

The Revised Common Lectionary assigns 2 Thessalonians 1:1–4, 11–12 for Proper 26, Year C. The excision of verses 5–10 diplomatically allows the preacher who wishes to do so to skip over the troublesome questions raised by those verses and their eternal damnation of unbelievers. Given the fact that verses 5–10 do make something of a digression from the thanksgiving proper, this particular bit of surgery makes more sense than many of the excisions made by the lectionary. A sermon on verses 1–4, 10–12 might well focus on the relationship between faith in the sense of belief and faith in the sense of faithfulness or explore the responsibility of "boasting" about God's work in the church.

The preacher needs to keep in mind, however, that curious worshipers may well read verses 5–10 for themselves, and here we encounter significant problems of interpretation. When the writer says that God is just to "repay with affliction those who afflict you" and that those who "do not know God" and who "do not obey the gospel of our Lord Jesus" will endure eternal destruction, the heart wilts. Perhaps at one time in North America, such language cheered on believers, for non-Christians inhabited some other continent on which most of us had never set foot and whose faces we could scarcely even imagine. Particularly those not accustomed to separating the context of 2 Thessaloni-

105

ans from the context of the present will think immediately of their Buddhist neighbors or agnostic daughter-in-law or Jewish teacher or lapsed Presbyterian brother.

How are such concerns to be addressed with care and without compromising the biblical text? To begin with, close and careful reading of the text in its context shows that this is less a reasoned analysis of who is "in" and who is "out" with God than an angry cry on behalf of a small and beleaguered community which knows God will not leave its suffering without answer. The language about destruction for these enemies yields to a different sort of language in verses 10–12, that of the joyous anticipation of Jesus' return and what that return will mean for the faithful.

In addition, perhaps more than a little caution is required. As Ebenezer Scrooge had to learn that he himself might be among the "surplus population," many of us might ask whether we can say that we have obeyed "the gospel of our Lord Jesus" (v. 8). By that criterion, heaven will be not only a vast but a vacant space.

The best clue to hearing this passage rightly in the present is to ask what word it says to and about believers, rather than what it says about anyone else. That is, the real question is what word is being addressed to us and not what is being said about others. With its rage against those who persecute the church comes the reminder of those many Christians for whom faithfulness did and does involve suffering. Second Thessalonians does not glorify suffering in and of itself, but it does acknowledge the suffering of this group of believers. It recognizes that the gospel is a demanding business. It is not a partial or part-time commitment, squeezed in among other activities or relegated to one day (even one scant hour) weekly. The gospel is nothing less than the central claim in the life of believers, who know that their lives are not their own.

Finally, this passage needs to be read in its context in the canon. This is not the Bible's only word about the future and salvation. Romans 8 anticipates the redemption of creation itself, and the tortured Paul of Romans 9—11 resolves his concern about Israel's rejection of its own Messiah with the words "And so all Israel will be saved" (11:26) and with praise for the mystery of God's judgment. In other words, some things (indeed, many things) are best left to God's own wisdom.

A different sort of canonical strategy would be to imagine what the author of 2 Thessalonians would say when confronted with Jesus' admonition, "[L]ove your enemies and pray for those who persecute you" (Matt. 5:44). Perhaps the best answer to that question lies in the discussion of the "lawless one" in chapter 2. For 2 Thessalonians, these afflictors of the faithful are not simply good people gone wrong, or even

106

very bad people. They are characters in a larger drama, very probably agents of Satan.

It is interesting to contemplate how the writer imagines the audience will hear this promise of vengeance. Clearly he is writing for believers. This is not an impassioned plea delivered by a street-corner preacher to persecutors who need to mend their ways. Neither is it a tract dedicated to the conversion of unbelievers. Presumably the writer hopes that the Thessalonians will draw comfort from this promise of a future in which their enemies will be overcome and they themselves will find relief.

The Return of the Lord and the Revelation of Evil

2 THESSALONIANS 2:1–17

Readers of the New Testament stumbling for the first time into the middle of 2 Thessalonians may be forgiven if they feel like Alice tumbling down a dark hole into Wonderland. The residents of this Wonderland are new and mysterious, their relationships to one another unclear, and the stranger responds with a sense of disorientation. Before abandoning this territory in dismay (or perhaps worse, prematurely attaching external identifications to the characters and events in the new territory), we need to chart a map that will give our explorations some landmarks.

In a way generally parallel to the first chapter of the letter, this one begins (vv. 1–2) and ends (vv. 13–17) with words of comfort for believers, and the central section (vv. 3–12) focuses on those outsiders who constitute a threat to the faithful. Verses 1–2 introduce the topic of the "day of the Lord" and emphatically insist that believers should not be disturbed by reports to the effect that it has already arrived. Verses 3–12 then explain in detail how the writer knows that the "day of the Lord" has not yet arrived and what must happen before that time can come. Verses 13–17 conclude with thanksgiving and prayer for the continued faithfulness of the Thessalonians in light of this situation.

Admittedly, it is far easier to analyze the general structure of this chapter than it is to understand its content. The brief synopsis of the preceding paragraph would give a newcomer no sense of what Alice will

107

find in this Wonderland, largely because the central section of this passage (vv. 3–12) actually consists of a small narrative, complete with new characters and a plot bearing its own struggle, defeat, and triumph. This particular narrative is not "Alice in Wonderland," but might better be called "The Defeat of Delusion."

In offering this story, the writer's strategy seems to stand in tension with itself. On the one hand, the writer wants to allay any fears that the "day of the Lord" has already begun, by pointing out that certain things must happen before that occasion arrives. On the other hand, however, the unfolding of events in verses 3–12 has a sense of urgency about it that suggests immediacy and might even bring about the anxiety he seeks to prevent.

Christians have puzzled over this passage since early in the church's life, and the technical commentaries on this letter chronicle those discussions in detail. It is best to admit at the outset that much in this section of the letter continues to be elusive. If Augustine was forced to concede, "I frankly confess I do not know what he means" (*City of God* 20.19), we should not be ashamed to do the same. We will trace the lines of the passage, not with the intent of "solving" a riddle, but with a view to grasping the dynamics of the story it tells and understanding the ways it might have addressed believers in a context of persecution as well as the ways it might be heard again in the present.

2 Thessalonians 2:1–2
Shaken Up by the
Day of the Lord

The order of phrases in the NRSV reverses the order in the Greek. "We beg you, brothers and sisters" stands at the beginning of the Greek, underscoring the importance of the new subject (see the similar openings in 1:3 and 3:1). What the writer endeavors to draw attention to is the compound subject that follows: "the coming of our Lord Jesus Christ and our being gathered together to him."

Apparently the Thessalonians already know what these phrases mean (see 2:5) so that no explanation of the subject itself is offered. As often in the New Testament, Jesus' return is referred to by the Greek word *parousia*, "coming" (see, for example, Matt. 24:3; 1 Cor. 15:23; James 5:7, 8). The second half of the subject is also a noun, *episynagōgē*, which is translated a bit awkwardly as "being gathered together." The NRSV assumes that this gathering recalls that comforting scene in 1 Thessalonians 4:17, in which all believers, both those who have died and those who remain alive, rise to be with Jesus, so it reads "gathered together *to him.*" But the Greek may also be rendered "gathered together *before him,*" in the sense that believers gather to witness and receive justice. Given the insistence in this letter on God's retributive justice, the second alternative seems more probable.

Whatever the connotation of the gathering, its prospect appears not joyous but in fact terrifying to the letter's recipients. They, or at least a number of them, are in danger of believing that "the day of the Lord is already here" (v. 2). Here we encounter one of the major historical questions regarding this letter: What exactly does such an assertion mean and what place does it have in the letter?

The language is unequivocal. To say that "the day of the Lord is already here" is not simply to say that it "will come" (as in 1 Thess. 5:2) or that it is "near" (as in Rom. 13:12). Other Greek expressions permit those translations, but this one does not. Indeed, Romans 8:38 carefully distinguishes between "things present" and "things to come," using an inflected form of the same Greek verb for those present things as the verb in our text. On the other hand, "the day of the Lord is already here" cannot mean that the Parousia itself had taken place, since the arrival of Jesus himself could scarcely be disputed.

It may be—and here we can only speak in the language of possibility—that the assertion means that certain things had happened that some believers associated with the arrival of the Parousia. They could have identified their own experience of suffering with those "tribulations" that were to precede the arrival of the Parousia. Since 1 Thessalonians itself speaks about "sudden destruction" in connection with the day of the Lord (5:2), Christians, either in Thessalonica or in another location at a later time, may have read their own situation in that letter, or it may be that a prophet has made the association on behalf of the community. However the proclamation has arisen, it threatens the community, perhaps even generating the idleness spoken about in 3:6–13.

Such outbreaks of apocalyptic frenzy dot the landscape of Christian history, and we do not require transportation into the first century to find them. Nor are they confined to Christian history. The first-century Jewish historian Josephus reports that, when the Roman army entered Jerusalem and was about to take over the Temple, many were falsely persuaded that this evil would require God's intervention. Rather than flee the Temple and even the city of Jerusalem itself, they rushed to the Temple precincts to witness God's great intervention

109

(*Jewish War* 6.284–87). It is only too easy to imagine that a calamity, particularly the deaths of Christians as a result of persecution, might have lit the fuse of apocalyptic terror.

In response, 2 Thessalonians urges believers "not to be quickly shaken in mind or alarmed." The NRSV's "shaken in mind" is a bit tepid; F. F. Bruce puts it better: "shaken out of your wits" (*1 and 2 Thessalonians*, 161). The writer makes the warning still more emphatic by specifying three ways in which such an alarmist report might reach them. It might arrive either "by spirit," presumably by a prophetic pronouncement, one that would need to be tested and found inadequate in this case (see 1 Thess. 5:19–21). It might also arrive "by word," which probably refers to the use of reason, to the "logical" deductions individuals might make based on events. Most curiously, the writer warns that it might arrive "by letter, as though from us." The addition of the phrase "as though from us" could mean that an individual or a group of believers was circulating this spurious pronouncement by means of a letter purporting to be from Paul. It may also mean that the author of 2 Thessalonians is attempting to cast doubt on the authenticity of 1 Thessalonians and its teaching about the unpredictability of the Parousia.

Probably few contemporary pastors (at least the pastors who would be reading this commentary) find themselves with parishioners who have been set atremble because of a prediction that the day of the Lord has already come, but most will have encountered those who are severely alarmed by some event—whether it is the local church's budget shortfall or the most recent round of denominational infighting or the ecological crisis. In such situations, restrained reflection is the first casualty of a fear that seems to feed upon itself. As any pastor would do, the author of 2 Thessalonians wants to forestall the consequences of this unleashed anxiety and attempts to counter it.

2 Thessalonians 2:3–12
The Defeat of Delusion

In an effort to calm the anxieties of his audience, the writer of 2 Thessalonians responds with a story. We will explore this story through its characters, its plot, and its use of time, before asking how it might function as a response to the anxiety introduced in verses 1–2.

The cast of characters supplied for this miniature story is dizzying. In addition to God and the Lord Jesus, it includes the rebellion, the law-

110

less one, the restrainer, the mystery of lawlessness, Satan, and those who are perishing. Although the rebellion and the mystery of lawlessness are not characters, strictly speaking, they become characters in this little narrative by virtue of being anthropomorphized (the "rebellion *comes first,*" and the "mystery of lawlessness *is already at work*" [emphasis added]). That strategy lends urgency and a sense of impending danger to the story.

The Lawless One

Because of the difficulties that plague attempts to identify them, the characters of the lawless one and the restrainer require careful attention. The characterization of the "lawless one" is ominous. "Rebellion" precedes this figure, preparing the way for him. Our English noun "apostasy" transliterates this Greek word, which almost certainly refers to religious rather than political rebellion (although the distinction between the two in the first century is not sharp). The context suggests that it is religious, because the activity of the lawless one (v. 4), which is so closely connected with this rebellion, is activity against God rather than against the state. A number of early Christian texts anticipate a period of rebellion that will precede God's final intervention in human history (see, for example, Matt. 24:6–14; 1 Tim. 4:1–4; 2 Tim. 3:1–5; Jude 17–19).

To say that the "lawless one" is religiously lawless probably does not mean laxity in the sense of disobedience to Jewish law. The controversies over Christian obligation to the Jewish law that figure prominently in some of the Pauline letters and the Acts of the Apostles do not play a role in 1 or 2 Thessalonians. Instead, lawlessness here is characterized by the refusal to submit to the authority of God as creator, the refusal to acknowledge God as God.

The "lawless one" is identified further as "the one destined for destruction," or literally, "the son of destruction." In biblical idiom, of course, the "son of" something is one who belongs to that realm. For example, the "sons [or children] of light" in 1 Thessalonians 5:5 are those who belong to the realm of the light. This lawless one, then, belongs to the power of destruction (see John 17:12, where Judas is called "the son of destruction").

Verse 4 describes the actions of this figure, actions that themselves disclose his character: "He opposes and exalts himself above every so-called god or object of worship, so that he takes his seat in the temple of God, declaring himself to be God." Several Old Testament passages influence this description. Daniel 11:36 speaks of the pretensions of Antiochus Epiphanes:

111

> The king shall act as he pleases. He shall exalt himself and consider himself greater than any god, and shall speak horrendous things against the God of gods. He shall prosper until the period of wrath is completed, for what is determined shall be done.

Similarly, Ezekiel 28:2 accuses the king of Tyre:

> [Y]ou have said, "I am a god;
> I sit in the seat of the gods,
>   in the heart of the seas,"
> yet you are but a mortal, and no god,
>   though you compare your mind
>   with the mind of a god.

And Isaiah 14:13 anticipates taunting the king of Babylon:

> You said in your heart,
>   "I will ascend to heaven;
> I will raise my throne
>   above the stars of God;
> I will sit on the mount of assembly
>   on the heights of Zaphon;
> I will ascend to the tops of the clouds,
>   I will make myself like the Most High."

When 2 Thessalonians looks for the arrival of a "lawless one" who exalts himself and declares himself God, the influence of these passages (whether conscious or unconscious) is obvious.

That influence means that the attempt to parse each element in this description is futile. In particular, commentators have sometimes fretted over the reference here to the Temple ("he takes his seat in the temple of God"). Some want to identify this reference with a particular occasion on which someone violated the Jerusalem Temple, such as when the Roman Emperor Caligula undertook to have a statue of himself installed. Others use this reference to date the letter, arguing that the letter must have been written before the Jerusalem Temple was destroyed in 70 C.E. However, the author may have in mind God's dwelling place in a heavenly temple (as in Ps. 11:4; see also Ps. 18:6; Isa. 66:1; Hab. 2:20), particularly in view of the claim that the lawless one attempts to unseat God.

The lawless one is often identified with the expectation of the Antichrist, although the author does not call him by that name. Only in the Johannine epistles do we find the word "antichrist" or "opposing Christ" (1 John 2:18, 22; 4:3; 2 John 7), although other New Testament texts provide evidence of an expectation that a figure or figures would arise against Jesus prior to the time of his Parousia (as in Matt. 24:5, 23–24; Mark 13:21–22; Luke 21:8; Revelation 13).

Even if 2 Thessalonians does not identify the lawless one explicitly as an antichrist or false Christ, the description carries motifs that are elsewhere associated with Jesus. Like Jesus Christ, the lawless one will be "revealed" when the time is right (v. 5, 6). Like Jesus, a "mystery" is associated with him (v. 7). Like Jesus, he will have a *parousia* (v. 9, "coming" in NRSV). To press the commonalities somewhat, the lawless one comes only after his predecessor, the rebellion, just as Jesus comes only after his predecessor, John the Baptist.

The quest to learn the name of this figure has proved irresistible to Christians across the centuries. Perhaps we sense that, if we have the Antichrist's name, we will have power over that figure as Jesus demanded the names of the evil spirits he ousted. Scholars, wanting to understand who the writer views as the lawless one, have proposed Belial, the Roman Empire, an unidentified false prophet, and even an incarnation of Satan. And in the millennia since 2 Thessalonians, other Christians have proposed everyone from the pope to Luther to the countries of the European common market to, very recently, Mikhail Gorbachev (as in the 1988 book, *Gorbachev! Has the Real Antichrist Come?*). The sheer number of these proposals should caution against the assumption that the identity of this figure can be determined. The author may have had a clear identification in mind for the "lawless one," but we cannot identify that person or figure at this distance.

The Restrainer

Over against this "lawless one" is the other highly elusive character in this chapter, the restrainer. (One of the many difficulties surrounding the interpretation of this character is that v. 6 refers to the *thing* [neuter] that is restraining and v. 7 to the *one* [masculine] who is restraining; the expression "the restrainer" is helpful because it encompasses both options.) Attempts to identify this restrainer are not quite so multitudinous as attempts to identify the lawless one, but they are just as futile. Some have argued that it must be God who reins in the power of lawlessness, until the time appointed for the last things has arrived. Others think that the restraining thing is the Roman Empire and the restraining person the emperor himself. On this view, the writer sees in the lawful government of the Roman Empire the constraint to evil; when that empire is removed, the forces of lawlessness will run unchallenged, signaling the onset of the Parousia. Still others contend that Paul perceives his own ministry as the force that holds off lawlessness; Paul works under such a sense of compulsion (as in 1 Cor. 9:16, for example) because he knows that the time is short. Others contend that we

113

cannot know who the restrainer (or the lawless one) is, because these events have not yet occurred.

As with the lawless one, the identity of the restrainer is utterly hidden from us. According to verse 6, the initial audience of this letter knew who it was. We do not. What we can learn, however, is what role the restrainer plays in the story and perhaps also how it functions in the author's strategy of comforting and strengthening this community of the faithful.

A Plot of Rebellion

Having examined the new characters in this story, we turn to its plot, which is simple and direct, at least on one level: As a result of the deceptive activity of Satan, lawlessness is already at work in the world. Something or someone is now restraining the full force of that lawlessness. At some future point, the restraining force will be set aside, full-scale rebellion will break out, and the lawless one will himself appear and challenge the rule of God. When that happens, the Parousia will take place and the Lord Jesus will destroy the lawless one with the very breath of his mouth. The "Cliff's Notes" version of this story might read as follows: Evil is powerfully at work in the world and will stage a final rebellion, but God's agent will defeat it.

This is a straightforward story of good and evil. What makes it complex, in addition to the mystery surrounding two of the characters, is that the writer does not narrate it straightforwardly. The writer moves back and forth in time. The miniature story that begins in verse 3 starts by pointing to the future; the day of the Lord will come in the future only after the rebellion and the arrival of the lawless one. Then the writer moves back to the present: The Thessalonians are to remember what they have already been told (v. 5); the restrainer is now at work (v. 6); lawlessness is already at work (v. 7). Verse 8 moves forward again into the future, where the story reaches its climax in Jesus' destruction of this lawless one. Then in verses 9–11 the writer returns to the present with the working of Satan and those who are perishing and with God's own act of deluding the perishing.

This interweaving of times is integral to the strategy of the passage. Before we consider that strategy, we need to linger over a few features of the story. Verse 8 exults in the fact that the returning Jesus will destroy the lawless one "with the breath of his mouth" (presumably playing on such Old Testament texts as Job 4:9; Ps. 33:6; and Isa. 11:4). Hollywood would not be at all happy with this detail of the story. No great force is needed to overcome this opponent. No special effects awards are imminent, for all that would be needed are the appearance of the Lord Jesus and his very breath. In other words, the power of evil, while it is real and great, is as nothing when face-to-face with the power of the only living God.

Deception and Delusion

Alongside this revealing way of speaking about the power of God stands the issue of deception and delusion. Verses 11–12 depict the plight of the "perishing" in terms that are frightening, perhaps even terrifying, for here the text asserts that it is *God* who deludes people. The logic turns on the claim that these are people who do not love (v. 10) or believe (v. 12) the truth. They are under the sway of Satan, whose modus operandi is deception (vv. 9–10). For that reason God sends a delusion, one that they will believe and that will lead to their condemnation.

Sorting through the assertions in this passage is a bit like separating strands in a bowl of cooked spaghetti. It bears a resemblance to other biblical passages in which God is said to send or speak a lie for God's own purposes (see, for example, 1 Kings 22:23; Ezek. 14:9). With its condemnation of those who prefer the lie (about their own autonomy) to the truth (that only God is God), it also recalls Romans 1:18–32 (see also 2 Tim. 4:4). Here the implacable human refusal to let God be God becomes quite specific. Not only will those who are perishing not permit God to be God, but they will also not believe the truth. Because they *will* believe lies, God sends them a lie. Verses 10–12 might be paraphrased, à la Romans 1: "Because they preferred delusion to the truth, God handed them over to every sort of delusion so that their condemnation might be complete."

Notice that deception is not only what Satan has done to the unrighteous, those who have not believed the truth, but also a very present danger within the community of faith: "Let no one deceive you in any way" (v. 3). The situation the writer confronts is a matter not simply of calming butterfly-ridden tummies but of combating a powerfully destructive evil.

The Power of Delusion

Probably the tension at work in this story between its frightening particulars and the desire to calm frightened wits has to do with the fact that the writer has two distinct but related targets in view. One target is explicit, and that is the anxiety of believers. The writer attempts to

115

address that anxiety by explaining that certain events must occur prior to the Parousia. Since those events have not yet taken place, or at least they have not been completed, there is no need for believers to panic.

Although the second target is not explicitly identified, there does seem to be one, namely, those who are afflicting the church. The persecution of believers is not mentioned in this passage either as a sign of the Parousia or as one of the symptoms of the arrival of the lawless one; particularly if the claim that the "day of the Lord is already here" is being linked to the present persecution of Christians, that silence is understandable. However, the way in which chapter 2 characterizes the doings of evil surely includes the persecutors of chapter 1. The "mystery of lawlessness" that is already underway necessarily includes those who refuse to know God and who afflict the faithful. The rage of chapter 1 against those who persecute believers has by no means dissipated; it has only been extended into the future.

By means of this brief narrative, the writer also reinforces and expands one of the central assertions of chapter 1: There will be an accounting. All those who are in rebellion against God will be condemned along with their master, Satan, because God will finally triumph. The interweaving of tenses in this story, and especially the use of the present tense, conveys the intrusion of evil and the threat of evil even in the present. Although the "day of the Lord" may not be at hand, the "mystery of lawlessness" is a present threat.

This may explain why the writer employs a story in response to the anxiety within his audience. What the story does is to make the danger of evil real. It also invites the hearers to know what that evil is and does and precisely how it will be defeated. The problem the particulars of the writer's strategy pose for later generations, who undertake to decode these details in order to learn when Jesus is coming back, should not prevent our paying adequate attention to the two prominent concerns in this passage—rebellion against God and delusion.

In the story of 2 Thessalonians 2, it is the figure of the "lawless one" who manifestly rebels against God by setting himself in the place of God (v. 4). Whether or not Christians still anticipate the arrival of such a figure, the assertions made here about the nature of rebellion remain powerful. They also should seem familiar, because rebellion against God continues to be the fundamental religious—indeed the fundamental human—error in that it denies the very "godness" of God. In this sense F. F. Bruce is right when he comments that our question regarding this passage ought not be who the "lawless one" is. Our question should instead be, "Lord, is it I?" (*1 and 2 Thessalonians*, 187).

The impulse to deny God's godliness, to deny that we are created and not creator, is an impulse deeply set within the human heart. Christians perceive it most easily in the "modern" notion that humankind has moved beyond the need for God. The explanatory power once vested in the biblical account of creation is no longer necessary, and so God is no longer necessary. The appeal to science only provides a recent variation on an ancient temptation, of course. There is nothing new about denying the existence of God, as a rereading of Psalm 14 will demonstrate.

Rebellion against God is not the unique preserve of the nonbeliever, however. It is also, perhaps especially, seen among the devoutly religious. Genuine belief in God's existence and the sincere desire to serve God rightly create an environment highly conducive to the growth of the assumption that one *knows* God's mind (perhaps even better than God does). Precisely by virtue of wishing to please God, the religious person is tempted to become God, to dictate God's terms to God. That form of rebellion against God is far more powerful than the denial of God, for it masks itself as obedience, even from the rebels themselves.

Delusion is intimately connected with rebellion against God, whatever form that rebellion takes. Rebellion occurs, not because individuals make a conscious decision to rebel against God, even though they know that only God is God and that they are God's creatures. They rebel because they are deluded into believing that they have no need of God or that they already know God's mind.

The notion of being in the grips of a delusion profoundly disconcerts us, as it should. When we say that someone is psychologically deluded, we suggest that she is out of touch with the real world. He believes himself to be Napoleon or Alexander the Great. She is convinced that she can cross the Grand Canyon with a single step. It is as if the deluded existed within some alien membrane, a membrane that is life-threatening but that cannot be penetrated. Theological delusions are perhaps less dramatic to the observer, but no less firmly entrenched. The deluded believes that hard work will always bring success, or that personal wealth creates personal security, or that religious behavior will guarantee God's favor.

According to this passage, both rebellion and delusion exist not simply because certain individuals or groups decide to rebel against God, but because of the "working of Satan." This assertion raises the important question of evil and the way it is discussed among Christians.

REFLECTION:

The Persistence of Evil

The drama of 2 Thessalonians 2:1–12 presents interpreters with a powerful temptation to concentrate on details at the expense of attending to larger theological concerns. Puzzling over what the author understands by "the rebellion," the "lawless one," and the "restrainer," as well as how these phenomena work together, can prove enormously stimulating. Wild speculations about exactly when the return of Jesus will occur or elaborate attempts to identify the "man of lawlessness" make for fascinating reading. As entertaining and even enlightening as these endeavors may be, they also serve to divert us from the text's insistence on the presence of evil in the world.

The vocabulary of evil pervades the passage. From the deception that threatens believers; to predictions of rebellion, destruction, and lawlessness; to the arrival of Satan himself, the writer heaps up imagery associated with evil. Although the language of evil dominates this particular passage, it occurs elsewhere in the letter as well. The writer anticipates judgment for those who afflict believers (1:5–12) and anticipates the rescue of believers from "wicked and evil people" (3:2). Given the brevity of the letter, the density of this language of evil becomes all the more striking.

Ironically, the Revised Common Lectionary includes none of these passages in its readings from 2 Thessalonians (all of which appear in Year C). The reading for Proper 26 jumps from 1:4 to 1:11, skipping over the promise of retribution. The reading for Proper 27 is 2:1–5, 13–17, omitting the reference to Satan and his works. The final reading is 3:6–13, so that the reference to "wicked and evil people" in 3:2 is likewise missing.

Those decisions are understandable, given the many difficulties of these passages and the capacity Christians (in common with the rest of humanity) have demonstrated for objectifying evil in the person of the outsider or the enemy. The decisions of the lectionary committee reflect something more than the avoidance of certain exegetical difficulties and sensitivity to history, however. They may also reflect unwillingness to acknowledge and face the presence of evil in the world.

The avoidance of evil manifests itself in a variety of ways in contemporary Christianity. Nearly twenty-five years ago, Karl Menninger
118 embarrassed the church with his famous title, *Whatever Became of Sin?* That his question has not received a satisfactory answer becomes

clear in congregations where the confession of sin in corporate worship has come under attack as inducing guilt or indicting all people needlessly. As one woman explained her refusal to sing "Amazing Grace": "I am not a wretch, I never was a wretch, and I do not see why I should sing that I was." We can only confess sin when we recognize it to be sin, and we can only recognize sin in the larger context of a sense of good and evil.

The price we pay for our unwillingness to speak and think about evil is high indeed. In his elegant and insightful book *The Death of Satan: How Americans Have Lost the Sense of Evil,* Andrew Delbanco chronicles the changing understandings of evil in American history. Delbanco argues that Americans have largely understood evil in a Manichaean sense as outside themselves, whether in the form of Satan, the racial or ethnic other, or the foreign enemy. Particularly in recent history, however, Americans have lost the sense of evil altogether; we have no language with which to talk about it because we have, in Richard Rorty's phrase, no "criterion of wrongness" (*Contingency, Irony and Solidarity,* 75). Delbanco argues for a renewed sense of evil, one informed by Augustine's understanding of evil as privation, as the capacity of the self to deny and reject the good.

Delbanco writes from a secularist position (although he recognizes that faith is still an option exercised by millions of Americans), but he nevertheless sees the recognition of evil as imperative. The specter he confronts is "that if evil, with all the insidious complexity which Augustine attributed to it, escapes the reach of our imagination, it will have established dominion over us all" (234).

Delbanco's insight has even more currency for those who operate within Christian tradition. The unwillingness to speak of evil has serious consequences for believers. To begin with, it means that we lose a vocabulary that allows us to address many pastoral concerns, both those of an individual and of a corporate nature. Those who watch loved ones struggle against cancer or mental illness may not resort to the language of "Satan and his minions," but they nevertheless know that they are witnessing a battle that is real and powerful. To speak of racism and its eradication only in terms of socialization and education constitutes a gross understatement of its force as evil and corrosive. However great the role of history in analyzing the tribal warfare in Eastern Europe or the Middle East, only the language of evil suffices to grasp after the intractable nature of those conflicts.

In addition to pastoral costs, the denial of evil has terrible consequences for theological anthropology, the theological understanding of

119

human nature. When we acknowledge the existence of evil in the world, we acknowledge our own limits, our own creatureliness. If there is no evil—if those "mistakes" we make occur *solely* because of flawed toilet training or repressive social forces—then we trick ourselves into imagining that we can overcome future "errors" through education or better socialization. Recognizing the reality of evil does not mean giving up on reform or giving up on human change, but it does mean acknowledging the human capacity for evil—*our* capacity for evil.

In the absence of a theological framework that acknowledges the human capacity for evil, how is it possible to talk about responsible behavior? Understanding the social and psychological factors that influence behavior is undeniably important, but such understanding can also be paralyzing if it is not accompanied by a call to responsibility, a call to shun evil and affirm good. This is the powerful contribution of Delbanco's book, which observes the "miraculous paradox" that it is the recognition of evil that demands the best of ourselves (something, as Delbanco observes, that "the devil himself could never have intended," 235).

In addition, the denial of the reality of evil has serious consequences for our understanding of God. When we shun talk about evil, in a sense we refuse to admit that God has enemies, and we thereby truncate our perception of God's power. This move happens often in the reading of passages such as 1 Corinthians 15, where Paul explicitly looks forward to the time when all God's enemies will be vanquished, even including the most powerful enemy, death itself. Readers who feel the need to "protect" God protest that God could not be engaged in battle with God's enemies, because there would be no need for such; God wins simply by entering the field. That view, however, misses a major dynamic in 1 Corinthians 15 (and in 2 Thessalonians and elsewhere): God's enemies are real and powerful, but God will be proved more powerful still (as God has already demonstrated in the resurrection of Jesus Christ). Ironically, then, our avoidance of evil does not purchase an understanding of God as good; it merely renders God the only power on the field.

Texts such as 2 Thessalonians 2:1–12, however they make us squirm, call us away from a white-bread Christianity, in which neither God nor the gospel has much depth or substance, to a recognition of the presence of evil in the world. They do not answer our questions about why evil exists, and they do not offer a talisman that protects us from its power or its consequences. Nevertheless, they do promise that the day will come when evil will be conquered, conquered by the mere breath of the Lord Jesus.

120

2 Thessalonians 2:13–17
Continuing in God's Calling

The small story at the center of 2 Thessalonians 2 is a story of God's triumph over all challengers, but it ends on a very somber note. It does not end with comfort but with yet another promise about what will happen to the enemies of the gospel (see 1:6–10). They will be condemned. From this awesome assertion to verse 13 seems a sharp transition. Suddenly the lens is focused once again, not on the lawless and those who are perishing, but on the Thessalonians. The transition is marked by an emphatic pronoun, "we," that sharply separates the Christian writer and other believers from those deluded souls in verses 11–12.

As in the initial lines of the letter, the author again comments on the necessity of thanksgiving ("we must always give thanks to God"). Thanksgiving is not a matter of civil or polite behavior (the religious equivalent of "Have a Nice Day!") but a fundamental obligation of human beings toward the God who created them (see on 2 Thess. 1:3). Here the thanksgiving focuses quickly on the audience.

The writer gives thanks "because God chose you as the first fruits for salvation through sanctification by the Spirit and through belief in the truth" (v. 13). If the previous lines have created the impression that believers are to be congratulated because they have escaped delusion by their own will or merit, this thanksgiving quickly reveals that to be a *mis*impression. It is God who "chose" believers for salvation and God who "called" them.

Specifically, believers were chosen to be "the first fruits." This phrase creates problems, particularly for interpreters who wish to affirm the Pauline authorship of this letter. Paul sometimes speaks of "first fruits" in reference to the first converts in a given region (as in Rom. 16:5; 1 Cor. 16:15), but the Thessalonians were not the first converts in Macedonia (see 1 Thess. 1:7–8; 2:2). Probably in this context, "first fruits" refers to the fact that these believers, whether in Thessalonica or elsewhere, are early among those Gentiles who believe the gospel and who know what the remainder of humankind will learn only at the Parousia. They are early among those set apart for salvation as the first fruits of a harvest were to be set aside for God (see Deut. 26:1–2). (As the footnote in the NRSV indicates, some Greek manuscripts of this letter read "from the beginning" instead of "first fruits.")

The two prepositional phrases at the end of verse 13 ("through sanctification by the Spirit and through belief in the truth") describe the means by which God's choice is experienced. The role of the Holy

Spirit in making believers themselves holy recalls 1 Thessalonians 4:3–8, where sanctification is identified as God's will for believers and God's gift of the Spirit is remembered.

The phrase "belief in the truth" both emphasizes the importance of faith (as in chapter 1) and contrasts this group with those just referred to—those who reject the truth and prefer the lie. Because Christians often want to transform faith into a new law that must be obeyed in order to achieve salvation, it is important to notice that in both verse 13 and verse 14 the initiative of God comes prior to sanctification and prior to belief. In other words, faith itself arises because God has granted it as a gift.

Verse 14 explains and further amplifies verse 13. "Through our proclamation of the good news" reminds the Thessalonians of the agency through which they became aware of God's call. That reminder also reinforces the authority of the apostles, an authority that will play an important role in the appeal to tradition in verse 15. The assertion "the glory of our Lord Jesus Christ" recalls 1:10, the culmination of the letter's depiction of the return of Jesus. Unlike those who will be forever alien from Christ's glory, believers will glorify the returning Christ and will be glorified together with him (1:12).

Verse 15 moves to draw an important conclusion from this thanksgiving: "So then, brothers and sisters, stand firm and hold fast to the traditions. . . . " The introductory words, "So then, brothers and sisters," already signal that the statement to follow is important. The imperatives that follow complement the warnings of verses 1–2. There the writer warned against being "quickly shaken in mind or alarmed," but now a positive assertion is made: "Stand firm and hold fast."

The fixture to which the Thessalonians are to cling is tradition, specifically, "the traditions that you were taught by us, either by word of mouth or by our letter." If tradition elsewhere in the New Testament carries sometimes a positive connotation (1 Cor. 11:2; Gal. 1:14) and sometimes a negative one (Matt. 15:3; Col. 2:8), here it is certainly positive. And it is specific in the sense that it is the traditions of these apostles that govern. In the context of the letter, that tradition appears to be the teaching about the day of the Lord (1:5—2:12) and the ethical instructions regarding work (2:6–13).

How is it possible for believers to "stand firm"? The answer to that question comes implicitly in the prayer-wish of verses 16–17. It is Jesus Christ and God who are the source of all comfort and strength. The order here ("our Lord Jesus Christ himself and God our Father") seems a bit unusual. Given the custom of the Pauline epistles and those of the Pauline school, we most often find the naming of God first and Christ second (for example, see Rom. 1:7; 1 Cor. 1:3; Eph. 1:2; Phil. 1:2; Philemon 3). Here the reversal of that practice may simply complement the order in verses 13–15, where God's activity precedes the reference to Christ.

Throughout this chapter, the writer has attempted to strengthen and comfort Christians who have been frightened out of their wits by false announcements of the day of the Lord. Finally, however, the acknowledgment comes that God is the one who grants comfort and hope and strength.

This section of 2 Thessalonians is fraught with peril for preachers and teachers. For understandable reasons, the Revised Common Lectionary includes verses 1–5 and 13–17 (for Proper 27, Year C) and diplomatically excises the most troublesome part of this text. To move from verse 5 to verse 13 without an intervening word of explanation renders the text sheer nonsense, however, and preachers who follow the lectionary closely might consider sermons on *either* verses 1–5 *or* 13–17.

Verses 1–5 might contribute positively to a frank discussion of alarmism in church life. This passage arises because someone has announced, like Henny Penny, that the sky is falling, and others have taken up the cry. Congregations abound with the heirs to this alarmist tendency. If they do not announce that the "day of the Lord is already here," they proclaim that the ordination of women will drive men from seminaries, that any change in the liturgy signals the onset of chaos, that the church will die out in this generation. Second Thessalonians 2 warns against the spiritual price paid by such alarmism and suggests that tradition and reasoned thought might serve to counter it.

Verses 6–12 should not be ignored, although this may be an instance where a sermon would either leave people scratching their heads or would include so much explanation that it would become unwieldy. Whether addressed in preaching or teaching, the insistence here on the power of evil *and* the immeasurably greater power of God needs to be recovered. Our discomfort with the apocalyptic characters in 2 Thessalonians 2 ought not render us mute regarding the ever present temptation to rebellion against God and to profound delusions about ourselves and our autonomy.

Verses 13–17 provide an important opportunity for reflection on that controversial word "tradition." For many contemporary Christians, tradition has become an albatross around the church's life; for many others, tradition is an endangered species. In adjudicating between these two extremes, it may prove instructive to consider the license with

123

which New Testament writers both appeal to and modify tradition. Even as Matthew punctuates his Gospel with a steady stream of quotations from Scripture (from tradition), he modifies those traditions by applying them to Jesus. The same free use of tradition occurs even in this passage, where the traditional expression "the day of the Lord" is applied to Jesus rather than to God, as *in tradition*. The question, then, is not whether tradition is albatross or endangered species, but how and why tradition is invoked and modified.

That little phrase in verse 14, "through our proclamation of the good news," stands as an important reminder for preachers themselves. God calls people to faith by a variety of means, and one of those means is preaching. Too often preachers persuade themselves that the task is outmoded, that no one listens, that preparation can be shortened and sloppy. Here we are faced with the claim that God works through that preaching to bring salvation into the lives of women and men. It cannot not be neglected.

The Things Commanded

2 THESSALONIANS 3:1–15

In view of the anger that permeates chapters 1 and 2 of this letter, the closing chapter is remarkable. Chapter 1 rages against those who afflict believers, anticipating the judgment that will fall on them. Chapter 2 interprets that rage in the larger context of rebellion against God: those who afflict believers are acting, not merely out of their own enmity, but out of the wrath of their superiors, evil and lawlessness themselves. They are the children of Satan, trapped by their own love of the lie. These elements are not missing in this final chapter. The writer seeks prayer so that the apostles may be rescued from "wicked and evil people; for not all have faith" (3:2). The Lord is recalled as the one who guards believers from "the evil one" (3:3). Those who are disobedient must be avoided (3:14).

Despite the continuing need to deal with evil and its threat of infiltration, the tone of the letter changes in this last chapter. The chapter begins with the anticipation that the "word of the Lord" will spread (3:1) and expresses confidence concerning both Jesus Christ and the Thessalonians (3:4). It concludes with words of peace from the one identified as "the Lord of peace." Enraged as the author is because of the trials of believers, that rage is not all that speaks, even in the midst of crisis.

The section begins with a prayer request, words of assurance, and a prayer-wish (vv. 1–6), followed by instructions on the disorderly (those "living in idleness," NRSV) and the treatment of those who persist in being disorderly (vv. 6–15). Throughout the passage, the writer focuses on the present time, whether it is the present of the mission, the present strength of believers in the face of evil, or the present conduct of those who are disorderly. This intense attention to the present supplements the strategy of 2:1–12 by directing the concerns of believers away from preoccupation with the eschaton and toward the immediate present and its demands.

2 Thessalonians 3:1–5
The Word of the Lord

This introductory section moves somewhat awkwardly from prayer request to prayer-wish. Initially, the writer seeks prayer for the apostles: "so that the word of the Lord may spread rapidly and be glorified everywhere." Literally, verse 1 desires that "the word of the Lord may run" (Gr. *trechō*) and recalls Psalm 147:15 ("his word runs swiftly"). The relationship between prayer *for the apostles* and the rapid movement *of the gospel* remains implicit rather than explicit, but the connection is surely that suggested by 2:14, that faith is awakened through the preaching of the gospel.

The "word of the Lord" does not run without encountering resistance. Although verse 2 provides no description or identifying characteristics for these "wicked and evil people," the reference to them already suggests that there are threats to the movement of the gospel. In addition, it recalls those in chapter 1 who are said to afflict believers and those in chapter 2 who are in rebellion against God. The Thessalonians share their affliction with the apostles themselves.

The awkward transition from verse 2 to verse 3 is more understandable if we notice that the two verses are connected by a word chain. The apostles are in danger because "not all have faith" (v. 2). Nevertheless, the Thessalonians may be confident because "the Lord is faithful" (v. 3). The difference in Greek between the words translated "faith" and "faithful" consists of a single letter, and the two words stand adjacent to one another in the Greek text ("for not all have faith. Faith-

125

ful is the Lord"). "Evil people" threaten the apostles (v. 2), but the Lord protects the Thessalonians from "the evil one" (v. 3).

The apparently gratuitous comment that "not all have faith" can be understood in at least two ways. It may have in view the request in verse 2 that the Thessalonians pray on behalf of the mission. In other words, the safety of the apostles is important because it is urgent that the gospel reach those who do not have faith. On the other hand, the admission that "not all have faith" can also refer to the comment that immediately precedes about "wicked and evil people." Although contemporary readers may cringe at the identification of unbelievers with evil, 2 Thessalonians seems to make that identification in 1:5–10, where "those who afflict you" and "those who do not know God" anticipate the same final judgment. Since the statement follows directly on the reference to "wicked and evil people," it is more natural to see it as a further comment on evil.

However "not all have faith" is construed, these "faithless" ones clearly trigger the reference to Christ's faithfulness in verse 3 (see also 1 Thess. 5:24). Whatever threat intrudes, the Lord will strengthen believers in the face of "the evil one." As the note in the NRSV indicates, there is ambiguity here. The Greek may be translated either as "the evil one" or "evil." Modern sensibilities may prefer the abstract "evil" to the notion of an "evil one," but the latter makes better sense in 2 Thessalonians with its earlier reference to Satan (2:9) and to the lawless one (2:3–4, 8–10). Other early Christian texts that refer to the devil or Satan in similar ways serve to reinforce this translation (see, for example, Matt. 13:19, 39; Eph. 6:16; 1 John 2:13, 14; and compare Matt. 6:13; John 17:15).

Readers of verse 4, especially those who are teachers or parents, may be excused for tossing a suspicious glance in the direction of the writer. Anyone who affirms confidence that "you are doing and will go on doing" what has been instructed (and then proceeds to give instructions!) sounds a little too much like the parent who insists that "I know you can do this task," or the teacher who encourages by saying, "What a great job you are doing!" To underscore that suspicion, we may ask, If the writer is so confident, why are these instructions even necessary?

In part, the answer to that question is that the confidence expressed here is a rhetorical device, just as it is when parents and teachers express confidence as a means of ensuring that their instructions will be followed. In addition, it is important to notice that the confidence is described as confidence "in the Lord." Consistent with the claim of verse 3 that the Lord is faithful, the writer knows that it is the Lord who enables believers to live as they should.

That confidence in the Lord is reaffirmed in the prayer wish of verse 5: "May the Lord direct your hearts to the love of God and to the steadfastness of Christ." As elsewhere in this letter, "the Lord" refers to the Lord Jesus Christ (1:2, 7, 8, 12; 2:1, 2, 8, 13, 14, 16), so that it may seem odd to pray that Christ would direct the hearts of the Thessalonians to the steadfastness of Christ. As in the language of strength in 2:17 and 3:3, this "direction" by the Lord counters the writer's concerns that the Thessalonians are being bounced about by every theological wind that blows.

What further secures the Thessalonians against evil is "the love of God" and "the steadfastness of Christ." In Greek each of these expressions is grammatically ambiguous. "Love of God" may be *either* human love for God (objective genitive) *or* God's love for human beings (subjective genitive). The Pauline letters and the Pauline tradition have little to say about humans loving God (see, for example, Rom. 8:28; 1 Cor. 8:3) and much to say about God's love for human beings (as in Rom. 5:8; 8:39; 2 Cor. 9:7; Eph. 2:4; Col. 3:12; 1 Thess. 1:4). In particular, 2 Thessalonians makes no other reference to human love for God, but it does speak of believers as loved by God (2:13, 16), making it likely that here as well what is desired is that believers concentrate on God's love for them.

Similarly, "steadfastness of Christ" can refer either to Christ's own steadfastness or to the steadfastness with which believers hope for Christ's Parousia (as in 1 Thess. 1:3). In the context of this letter, which seeks to correct a misplaced certainty about exactly when Christ will return, it is unlikely that the writer would open the door again to intensive eschatological expectation. Probably "steadfastness" here is a reminder of the afflictions endured by Christ, a reminder that may serve to embolden the letter's recipients.

2 Thessalonians 3:6–15
A Solemn Warning about Idleness

Second Thessalonians now takes up the problem raised by the behavior of some in the community who "are living in idleness and not according to the tradition that they received from us." In response, the writer begins (v. 6) and ends (vv. 14–15) with instructions that others need to avoid these persons. Sandwiched between these warnings are appeals to the pattern set by the apostles (vv. 7–9) and direct commands about labor (vv. 10–13).

With its solemn and formal tone, the opening of the passage signals that the writer regards the topic as one of grave importance: "Now we command you, beloved, in the name of our Lord Jesus Christ." The language of command has already appeared in verse 4, but there the rhetoric of confidence gentled it a bit. Here the gloves have been removed. The apostles have authority to command believers, and that authority comes to center stage in this verse. It returns again in verses 10 and 12, complemented by the reference to obedience in verse 14, so there is no overlooking its significance in this part of the letter.

This language of commandment is reinforced at the outset by appeal to the "name of our Lord Jesus Christ." This same phrase appears only once earlier in the letter, but its usage there is instructive. Following the depiction of the retribution to come at the Parousia and the subsequent glorification of the Lord Jesus, the writer prays that the Thessalonians may prove worthy of their calling so "that the name of our Lord Jesus may be glorified in you, and you in him." (1:12). If the goal of the Christian is to live so that the name of Jesus is glorified, then appeal to the name at the beginning of an ethical admonition indicates the high seriousness of the instruction that follows.

The instructions themselves make it clear that some of the Thessalonians have withdrawn from self-support through labor. The writer explicitly invokes the example of the apostles who "did not eat anyone's bread without paying for it" (v. 8) and refers to those who are unwilling to work. In language reminiscent of 1 Thessalonians 4:11, the writer insists that such persons work to support themselves (v. 12).

What is at issue here is something other than an early form of the Protestant work ethic, however. As in 1 Thessalonians 5:14, the NRSV translates "living in idleness" where "living in disorder" or "being disruptive" would be better (vv. 6, 11). Similarly, verse 7 should be "we were not disruptive" or "we were not disorderly," rather than "we were not idle." Although the refusal to work appears to be one of the leading problems with these believers, the word itself suggests something other than sloth; it suggests a sense of insubordination that results in disorderliness—and therefore includes a refusal to work (see above on 1 Thess. 5:12–24).

As a result of this disorderliness, such people are labeled "mere busybodies," people who occupy themselves with other people's business rather than their own. The Greek of verse 11 employs a delightful play on words that does not translate well into colloquial English. Literally, the Greek refers to those who are "not working but working

128

around." They do not do their own work, but they busy themselves with the work of other people. (For examples, see Demosthenes, *Orations* 26.15; 32.28; Polybius, *History* 18.51.2; Theophrastus, *Characters* 13.)

What motivates this pattern of disruptive behavior, in which some decide that they will no longer work but will work at meddling in the lives of others? The writer does not provide an explanation, but the most obvious possibility is that apocalyptic frenzy has triumphed over responsible behavior. Those who are convinced that "the day of the Lord is already here" (2:1) might well conclude that the time for work has yielded to the time for enthusiastic proclamation and warning. (Their neighbors might be forgiven for regarding this enthusiasm as something very much like meddling!)

The recent resurgence of interest in the social setting of early Christianity has prompted another suggestion about this passage. Some argue that those who refuse to work do so, not because they are convinced that the eschaton is at hand, but because they are poor and expect others to support them indefinitely. If this were the case, however, we might well find the author making the same sort of appeal to the judgment of outsiders that Paul makes in 1 Thessalonians 4:12.

Whatever the cause of this behavior, the writer employs a variety of strategies in response: appeal to tradition in the form of apostolic behavior, direct command to the disorderly to work, direct command to those who *are* orderly to persist in that behavior, and warning of isolation by the remainder of the community.

An Appeal to Tradition

The appeal to tradition is striking. Elsewhere in the Pauline corpus, tradition refers to early proclamation of the resurrection (1 Cor. 15:3, where "handed on" translates the Greek verb *paradidōmi*, "hand on as tradition") or to traditions regarding worship (1 Cor. 11:23; 15:2). Here, by contrast, tradition has become a specific practice of the apostles themselves and the necessity for other believers to imitate that practice.

In addition, the call for imitation here refers to a very specific behavior, that of the labor of the apostles. In the Pauline letters, the plea for believers to imitate Paul is often a general plea for believers to have the same values and perspectives as Paul (as in 1 Cor. 4:16; 11:1; Phil. 3:17; 4:9). First Thessalonians 1:6 does speak more specifically about imitation, but there, rather than urging imitation, Paul is recalling how the Thessalonians became imitators of the apostles' joy in the face of persecution (see also 1 Thess. 2:14).

129

In 2 Thessalonians 3:7–9, the writer seems to make explicit a call for imitation that is implicit in 1 Thessalonians. There, in the description of apostolic conduct, Paul recalls that "we worked night and day, so that we might not burden any of you while we proclaimed to you the gospel of God." This reminder of the initial visit anticipates Paul's exhortation regarding work in 4:11 (and possibly 5:14 also). In 2 Thessalonians, by contrast, the writer leaves no margin for misunderstanding but insists straightforwardly that this was done "to give you an example to imitate" (v. 10).

The appeal to tradition concludes with the reminder of instruction already given: "Anyone unwilling to work should not eat" (v. 10). The language employed is quite emphatic, referring to the presence of the apostles with the believers and using the language of command. Neither the Gospels nor the Pauline letters contain any such "commandment," and it may be that the writer draws on proverbial wisdom that has developed from Genesis 3:17–19 (see also Ps. 128:2 and Prov. 6:6–11). The *Didache*, an early Christian manual of instruction, reflects a similar wisdom: "[N]o Christian shall live idle in idleness. But if anyone will not do so [i.e., work], that person is making Christ into a cheap trade; watch out for such people" (12: 4–5; author's translation).

On the basis of this tradition, the writer directly addresses those who are "not doing any work" (v. 12). The language is strong. Not content with *either* "command" *or* "exhort," the writer uses both. Again, as in the introduction in verse 6, the appeal is made "in the Lord Jesus Christ." These disruptive persons are to "do their work quietly and to earn their own living." The second phrase, rendered more literally, is "Let them eat their own bread," which recalls Genesis 3:19 with its edict to Adam and Eve, "By the sweat of your face you shall eat bread."

If the transgressors are ordered in no uncertain terms, those who have remained faithful to the apostolic practice are also encouraged: "Brothers and sisters, do not be weary in doing what is right" (v. 13). This general admonition to do "what is right" might refer to any number of things or to Christian behavior generally. In this context, however, it almost certainly figures as a warning to those who have continued to work and remain orderly lest they find themselves attracted to the practices of others.

Avoiding the Disobedient (vv. 14–15)

The writer goes well beyond this gentle reminder to continued faithfulness, however. As noted earlier, the passage both begins (v. 6) and ends

(vv. 14–15) with the demand that those who persist in disorderly behavior are to be avoided. Contemporary readers may be puzzled, even mystified, by such counsel, but it has parallels elsewhere in the New Testament. In 1 Corinthians 5:3–5, Paul demands the "destruction of the flesh" (a much-debated phrase) for the believer who has been living with his father's wife. Second Corinthians 2:5–11 anticipates the forgiveness and restoration to the community of one who has been excluded for mistreatment of Paul. Matthew 18:15–18 instructs the church to exclude one who persists in sin ("let such a one be to you as a Gentile and a tax collector"; see also 1 Tim. 5:20). All of these passages reflect a concern for the boundaries of the community; if all behavior is tolerated, then the community of believers will cease to have any definition or meaning whatsoever.

The qualifying remark in verse 15 is significant: "Do not regard them as enemies, but warn them as believers." The exclusion of these disorderly Christians has the goal of warning them and making them ashamed (v. 14), presumably with the hope that they will be restored to the majority. Under no circumstances are they regarded as enemies. However mistaken these individuals may be in their conduct, they are not the enemies of the church. Second Thessalonians knows very well that the church has enemies (see 1:3–12!) and does not want the "out of order" believer understood in that way.

The emphatic and direct character of this exhortation in verses 6–15 is unmistakable. If only the possibilities for preaching the passage constructively were as obvious as the writer's rhetoric!

Throughout this brief letter, the writer has been insisting that believers have not yet left "the real world." The day of the Lord has not yet come. Believers live in peril from the church's enemies (1:4, 6–7) and from the reign of lawlessness itself (2:3). This passage develops that theme by insisting that believers have not left the world of responsibility. They must continue to work in order to provide for themselves. Although occasionally Christian groups do arrive on the scene with expectations about the imminent return of Jesus, our refusal to be responsible more often takes other forms. The irresponsibility of some believers probably finds its closest counterpart, not in our refusal to be responsible for our own food (we are quite vigilant on that point!), but in our refusal to be responsible for anything or anyone beyond ourselves. Much frenzy in contemporary Christianity is not eschatological frenzy that denies the importance of the "here and now" but frenzied building for "here and now" that denies the importance of the future.

Some will be tempted to hear the command "Anyone unwilling to work should not eat" as an inviting slogan for a new social policy. Those

131

who wish to render this bit of proverbial wisdom into a rule of law pro-
scribing the care of human beings for one another need to remember
that this is not the only word in the canon about how people are to be
fed. It is one thing to say that idle people should get back to work, but
the unmistakable message of the Bible is that humankind rightly hon-
ors its creator only when it also protects all those made and loved by
that same creator.

The Revised Common Lectionary lists verses 6–13 as the epistle
for Proper 28, Year C, carefully omitting verses 14–15 with their harsh
language about avoiding those who do not conform to the writer's
teaching about work. The omission is understandable, for many will re-
coil from the notion of excluding people, particularly given the way
such exclusions have been practiced in certain eras of Christian history.
The verses could, however, challenge the contemporary church to examine whether we are sufficiently committed to the gospel and to one
another to confront one another about matters of responsible living. Do
we avoid such confrontations because we fear being judgmental, or do
we use judgmentalism as an excuse for what is really nothing more than
indifference? The question is, Do we care enough about our fellow
Christians to challenge their behavior and to listen when they need to
challenge ours in turn?

"Do not regard them as enemies." This final warning sounds a particularly poignant note in the current climate of ecclesiastical wars. For
too many issues, Christians have divided up sides as if for a children's
game or, perhaps more accurately, for deadly confrontation. Denominational gatherings make the front page of daily newspapers, not because those gatherings witness to the gospel of Jesus Christ, but because the smell of blood attracts journalists. All too readily we think of
those who disagree with us as our enemies. They are not enemies, reminds 2 Thessalonians, but believers in need of correction.

Peace at All Times
in All Ways

2 THESSALONIANS 3:16–18

The direct warnings of 3:6–15 yield to conventions of a letter closing: the prayer-wish for peace (v. 16), the greeting (v. 17), the grace (v.
18). Although the Pauline letters regularly include a prayer for peace in

their conclusions (Rom. 15:33; 2 Cor. 13:11; Phil. 4:9; 1 Thess. 5:23), this one is remarkable for its completeness. Not only does it invoke the "Lord of peace" but wishes for "peace at all times in all ways." It also recalls the opening greeting of the letter: "Grace to you and peace from God our Father and the Lord Jesus Christ" (1:2). Whatever the faithful endure in the present, whatever rebellion and lawlessness threaten them in the future, and whatever perils exist because of their own disorder, they confidently expect to receive the gift of peace from the only one who is able to provide it.

The comment "This is the mark in every letter of mine; it is the way I write" is also extraordinary. Although Paul sometimes closes a letter with his own signature (see 1 Cor. 16:21; Gal. 6:11; and compare Col. 4:18), nowhere else do we find such insistence that this "is the mark in every letter of mine; it is the way I write." This unusual remark could mean that there has been a controversy about a forgery, and Paul seeks to reassure the Thessalonians that this letter is reliably his own (see 2:2). On the other hand, the reference to "every letter of mine" is hard to understand if Paul wrote this letter only a short time after 1 Thessalonians, thought to be Paul's earliest letter. This may be an indication that someone, probably someone who had been associated with Paul during his lifetime, wrote this letter and deliberately called attention to the greeting in order to ensure the favorable reception of the letter (see the discussion of this issue in the Introduction).

With the grace in verse 18, the letter comes to an end. Although this is a conventional element, it is not to be overlooked. Grace extends to "all of you," just as the writer invoked the Lord's presence with "all of you" in verse 16. In the light of the call for separation from the disorderly in verses 6–15, these references to "all" take on particular significance. Despite the need to confront and to discipline, the writer extends the profoundest of greetings to all believers.

BIBLIOGRAPHY

For Further Study of 1 and 2 Thessalonians

Best, Ernest. *A Commentary on the First and Second Epistles to the Thessalonians.* Harper's New Testament Commentaries. New York: Harper & Row, 1972.

Bruce, F. F. *1 and 2 Thessalonians.* Word Biblical Commentary. Waco, Tex.: Word Books, 1982.

Collins, Raymond. *The Birth of the New Testament: The Origin and Development of the First Christian Generation.* New York: Crossroad, 1993.

————. *Studies on the First Letter to the Thessalonians.* Bibliotheca ephemeridum theologicarum lovaniensium, 66. Louvain: Leuven University Press, 1984.

————, editor. *The Thessalonian Correspondence.* Bibliotheca ephemeridum theologicarum lovaniensium, 87. Louvain: Leuven University Press, 1990.

Donfried, Karl, and I. Howard Marshall. *The Theology of the Shorter Pauline Epistles.* New Testament Theology. Cambridge: Cambridge University Press, 1993.

Frame, J. E. *A Critical and Exegetical Commentary on the Epistles of Paul to the Thessalonians.* International Critical Commentary. Edinburgh: T. & T. Clark, 1912.

Jewett, Robert. *The Thessalonian Correspondence: Pauline Rhetoric and Millenarian Piety.* Philadelphia: Fortress Press, 1986.

Juel, Donald H. *1 Thessalonians.* Augsburg Commentary on the New Testament. Minneapolis: Augsburg Publishing House, 1985.

Krentz, Edgar M. "First and Second Epistles to the Thessalonians." *Anchor Bible Dictionary,* edited by David Noel Freedman, 6:515–23. New York: Doubleday & Co., 1992.

Malherbe, Abraham J. *Paul and the Thessalonians: The Philosophic Tradition of Pastoral Care.* Philadelphia: Fortress Press, 1987.

Marshall, I. Howard. *1 and 2 Thessalonians.* New Century Bible Commentary. Grand Rapids: Wm. B. Eerdmans Publishing Co., 1983.

Morris, Leon. *The First and Second Epistles to the Thessalonians.* New International Commentary on the New Testament, revised edition. Grand Rapids: Wm. B. Eerdmans Publishing Co., 1991.

Richard, Earl. *First and Second Thessalonians.* Sacra Pagina, 11. Collegeville, Minn.: Liturgical Press, 1995.

Wanamaker, Charles A. *The Epistles to the Thessalonians: A Commentary on the Greek Text.* New International Greek Testament Commentary. Grand Rapids: Wm. B. Eerdmans Publishing Co., 1990.

Other Works Cited in the Commentary

Adler, Mortimer. *How to Read a Book: The Art of Getting a Liberal Education.* New York: Simon & Schuster, 1940.

Anselm. *The Prayers and Meditations of Saint Anselm.* Translated by Benedicta Ward. London: Penguin Books, 1973.

Apostolic Fathers. Translated by Kirsopp Lake. Vol. 1. Loeb Classical Library. Cambridge, Mass.: Harvard University Press, 1912.

Augustine. *The City of God.* New York: Modern Library, 1950.

Aus, Roger D. "The Liturgical Background of the Necessity and Propriety of Giving Thanks according to 2 Thes 1:3." *Journal of Biblical Literature* 92 (1973): 432–38.

Bassler, Jouette M. "Peace in All Ways: Theology in the Thessalonian Letters. A Response to R. Jewett, E. Krentz, and E. Richard." In *Pauline Theology*, vol. 1, edited by Jouette M. Bassler, 71–85. Minneapolis: Fortress Press, 1991.

Bradley, Keith R. "Wet-Nursing at Rome: A Study in Social Relations." In *The Family in Ancient Rome: New Perspectives*, edited by Beryl Rawson, 201–29. Ithaca, N.Y.: Cornell University Press, 1986.

Castelli, Elizabeth A. *Imitating Paul: A Discourse of Power.* Literary Currents in Biblical Interpretation. Louisville, Ky.: Westminster/John Knox Press, 1991.

Charlesworth, James H., editor. *The Old Testament Pseudepigrapha*, 2 vols. New York: Doubleday & Co., 1983, 1985.

Chrysostom, John. *Homilies on Galatians, Ephesians, Philippians, Colossians, Thessalonians, Timothy, Titus, and Philemon.* Translated by G. Alexander, John A. Broadus, and Philip Schaff. Nicene and Post-Nicene Fathers, vol. 13. Grand Rapids: Wm. B. Eerdmans Publishing Co., 1988.

Cicero. *On Duties.* Translated by Walter Miller. Loeb Classical Library. Cambridge, Mass.: Harvard University Press, 1913.

Delbanco, Andrew. *The Death of Satan: How Americans Have Lost the Sense of Evil.* New York: Farrar, Straus & Giroux, 1995.

Dio Chrysostom. *Discourses.* Translated by J. W. Cohoon and H. Lamar Crosby. 5 vols. Loeb Classical Library. Cambridge, Mass.: Harvard University Press, 1932–51.

Fiore, Benjamin. *The Function of Personal Example in the Socratic and*

Pastoral Epistles. Analecta Biblica, 105. Rome: Biblical Institute Press, 1986.

Gaventa, Beverly Roberts. "Apostles as Babes and Nurses in 1 Thessalonians 2:7." In *Faith and History in the New Testament: Essays in Honor of Paul W. Meyer,* edited by John T. Carroll, Charles H. Cosgrove, and E. Elizabeth Johnson, 193–207. Atlanta: Scholars Press, 1991.

————. "The Maternity of Paul: An Exegetical Study of Galatians 4:19." In *The Conversation Continues: Studies in Paul and John in Honor of J. Louis Martyn,* edited by Robert T. Fortna and Beverly R. Gaventa, 189–201. Nashville: Abingdon Press, 1990.

————. "Our Mother St. Paul: Toward the Recovery of a Neglected Theme." *Princeton Seminary Bulletin* 17 (1996): 29–44.

Gillespie, Thomas W. *The First Theologians: A Study in Early Christian Prophecy.* Grand Rapids: Wm. B. Eerdmans Publishing Co., 1994.

Grenfell, Bernard P., editor. *The Oxyrhynchus Papyri.* Vol. 1. London: Egypt Exploration Fund, 1898.

Josephus. *Jewish Antiquities, Books XV–XVII.* Translated by Ralph Marcus and Allen Wikgren. Loeb Classical Library. Cambridge, Mass.: Harvard University Press, 1963.

————. *The Jewish War.* 2 vols. Translated by H. St. J. Thackeray. Loeb Classical Library. Cambridge, Mass.: Harvard University Press, 1927–28.

————. *The Life; Against Apion.* Translated by H. St. J. Thackeray. Loeb Classical Library. Cambridge, Mass.: Harvard University Press, 1926.

Juel, Donald H. "The Strange Silence of the Bible." *Interpretation* 51 (1997): 5–19.

Juvenal and Persius. *The Satires of Juvenal and Persius.* Revised edition. Translated by G. G. Ramsay. Loeb Classical Library. Cambridge, Mass.: Harvard University Press, 1940.

Käsemann, Ernst. "The Saving Significance of the Death of Jesus in Paul." In *Perspectives on Paul,* translated by Margaret Kohl, 32–59. Philadelphia: Fortress Press, 1971.

Krentz, Edgar. "Through a Lens: Theology and Fidelity in 2 Thessalonians." In *Pauline Theology,* vol. 1, edited by Jouette M. Bassler, 53–62. Minneapolis: Fortress Press, 1991.

Lutz, Cora. *Musonius Rufus: "The Roman Socrates."* Yale Classical Studies, 10. New Haven, Conn.: Yale University Press, 1947.

Malherbe, Abraham J. "'Gentle as a Nurse': The Cynic Background to I Thess ii." *Novum Testamentum* 12 (1970): 203–17.

Meeks, Wayne A. *The First Urban Christians.* New Haven, Conn.: Yale University Press, 1983.

Olbricht, Thomas H. "An Aristotelian Rhetorical Analysis of 1 Thessalonians." In *Greeks, Romans, and Christians: Essays in Honor of Abraham J. Malherbe,* edited by David L. Balch, Everett Ferguson, and Wayne A. Meeks, 216–36. Minneapolis: Fortress Press, 1990.

Philo. *Philo.* Translated by F. H. Colson, G. H. Whitaker, and J. W. Earp. 10 vols. Loeb Classical Library. Cambridge, Mass.: Harvard University Press, 1929–62.

Plutarch. "How to Tell a Flatterer from a Friend." *Plutarch's Moralia,* translated by F. C. Babbitt, vol. 1, 263–395. Loeb Classical Library. Cambridge, Mass.: Harvard University Press, 1928.

———. "Letter to Apollonius." *Plutarch's Moralia,* translated by F. C. Babbitt, vol. 2, 105–213. Loeb Classical Library. Cambridge, Mass.: Harvard University Press, 1928.

Rorty, Richard. *Contingency, Irony and Solidarity.* Cambridge: Cambridge University Press, 1989.

Seneca. *Ad Lucilium Epistulae Morales.* Translated by Richard Gunmere. 3 vols. Loeb Classical Library. Cambridge, Mass.: Harvard University Press, 1917, 1920, 1925.

Tacitus. *Histories IV–V; Annals I–III.* Translated by C. H. Moore and J. Jackson. Loeb Classical Library. Cambridge, Mass.: Harvard University Press, 1931.

Velleius Paterculus. *Compendium of Roman History.* Translated by F. W. Shipley. Loeb Classical Library. Cambridge, Mass.: Harvard University Press, 1924.

Vermes, Geza, translator and editor. *The Dead Sea Scrolls in English.* 3d ed. London: Penguin Books, 1987.